ST. JOSEPH
CATHOLIC MANUAL

**A Handy Digest of Principal Beliefs,
Popular Prayers, and Major Practices**

●

*With Complete References
to the
Catechism of the Catholic Church*

By

Rev. Thomas J. Donaghy

Illustrated

CATHOLIC BOOK PUBLISHING CO.
New York

NIHIL OBSTAT: Francis J. McAree, S.T.D.
Censor Librorum

IMPRIMATUR: ✠ Patrick J. Sheridan, D.D.
Vicar General, Archdiocese of New York

5 6 7 8 9 10 11 12 13 14 15

CONTENTS

PART 3: MAJOR PRACTICES

INTRODUCTION

THIS book is intended to be a constant companion for every Catholic and a substantial resource for those interested in or preparing to enter the Catholic Church. In a busy world, it offers a digest of the most important Catholic beliefs, the most popular Catholic prayers, and the most prominent Catholic practices.

In essence, it is a kind of modern Catechism. Naturally, it does not include everything that the *Catechism of the Catholic Church* does. But it does offer the basics of the faith found in that volume.

From another point of view, this book makes available the essentials of our Catholic culture. By reading it carefully, readers will become imbued with the Catholic outlook on life and on God.

At the same time, this book also presents ways in which readers can apply their faith—through prayers and practices that are beneficial to them.

In order to make the Manual even more helpful to our readers, we have printed in the margin the numbers of the *Catechism of the Catholic Church* where the themes may be found. This is true of any beliefs, prayers, or practices. By consulting the numbers in question, our readers can receive a fuller treatment of any topic mentioned herein.

It is the hope of both author and publisher that this Manual will enable Catholics to know, love, and live their faith. In this way, they will be what the name *Christians* stands for—true followers of Christ.

Introduction

1, 26, 1691

HUMAN beings act in accord with the beliefs they hold dear. Actions follow beliefs. If we truly believe a certain food is good for us, we will usually eat it. If we truly believe a certain book is beneficial for us, we will most likely read it.

The important phrase here is *truly believe.* Beliefs that are passing have no real say in what we do. Only those beliefs that are cherished by us influence our lives.

As Catholics, we have embraced a certain culture, a manner of thinking and acting that should become part of our way of life. But to live as Catholics, we must understand the beliefs the Church holds for us.

Once we have done that, we can put these beliefs into practice in our lives. This first part of the book is intended to set forth in summary form the most important teachings of the Church—the truths we believe.

"I Believe in God"

Searching for God

26-38, 144

OUR Faith or belief in God is rooted in our human awareness that we are a mystery to ourselves, that our whole life is permeated with a restlessness, a seeking that will not allow us to be at ease until our search for God has been fulfilled. In faith we believe that God has revealed certain truths to us. And these truths are bound up with our finding a solution to or a way out of our restlessness.

Accordingly, we begin to search out God's relationship with humanity. We scan recorded history for evidence of God in touch with His people. We discover Abraham, the

Israelites who were set free from captivity, John the Baptist preaching shortly after the division of Herod the Great's kingdom, the Jesus Whom John the Baptist preached, and the Jesus Who died for the salvation of mankind, and Who was raised by God from the dead that the gates of heaven might be opened.

50-67, 101 God's Revelation in Scripture

This history of God relating to human beings constitutes truths that God has revealed to us. In faith, we accept God's revelation. Just as in purely human affairs, we must rely on faith. For instance, when we are crossing a street or driving, we believe others will take the means to avoid entangling with us. If we hear there is a large city in Europe called Rome, we believe it even though we have never been there. We take it on faith, on another's word along with accepted evidence that such is the case.

Still, it is not enough to hold as true the truths of faith. For faith to be complete, its truths must bring us into a more personal relationship with God. It is important for us, therefore, to live according to what we believe of God. Like Abraham, despite all the human obstacles we may encounter, we accept God's promise of salvation, and we trust that no matter what difficulties, demands, or challenges we meet in opposition to our faith, we must, like Jesus, remain faithful and obedient to God in all our ways and works.

Jesus Christ embodies for us the very revelation of God. Our acceptance of Jesus is paramount. It is true that God has revealed Himself through the Prophets in the Old Testament and through Jesus Christ and the Apostles in the New Testament. The Old Testament idea of the word of God is understood by obedience in faith to His word. God revealed Himself in Adam and after him in Noah, Abraham, Daniel, and many other Prophets. Following Jesus and the Apostles, the Fathers of the Church illuminated revelation with a well-formulated insight into God's revealed truths.

Scripture and Tradition   75-83

And as we were reminded by Vatican Council II's *Dogmatic Constitution on Divine Revelation,* there is a significant close connection and communication between Sacred Tradition and Holy Scripture. Both flow from the same divine source, and their unity focuses on the same goal. This is why our understanding of faith should open God's people to the total and radical acceptance of the content and message of the Gospel. In reality, according to St. Thomas Aquinas, faith is simple, for it is our conversion to and belief in God.

"The Father Almighty"

198-260

God and Nature

OUR conversion to and belief in God, is as St. Thomas says, rooted in simple faith. Yet our experience of God is really a symbolic understanding. We do not experience God face to face, but at the same time, we are able to say something about God. And in speaking of God we reflect what are for us symbols or signs that we attribute to God.

However, when our social world changes we get new approaches to the signs we use to comprehend God in a limited way and in our understanding of God in His relationship to us. For example, in one stage of our history nature was thought to be sacred and was construed as a symbolic medium of the Divine World, God present to Himself.

With the growth of discovery, the emergence of nations, economic growth, development of new languages, the social upheaval of the Protestant reformation, and the new scientific age, along with the rise of individualism, nuanced signs or attributes of God surfaced.

Lawgiver and Supreme Being   199

Advances in science enabled humanity to move from a universe of mysterious change to one of law. People began to see

God as rational, the great architect, the master builder. This God of the Enlightenment likewise was considered to be abstract and distant, while, at the same time, revealing Himself in an ordered nature.

Individuals of faith saw God as a Supreme Being, one Who made the world, the laws of physics, while likewise establishing moral laws in His people. These latter laws have to be obeyed, and after death we are subject to reward or punishment. In our judgment before God all people are equal.

232-260 **Almighty and Father**
2779-
2793   In the process of rooting the signs of God in our thinking, we rely on both faith and reason. We move from faith to an Unmoved Mover; from an awareness of the tentativeness of our personal selves and others to a Necessary Being; and from unreasonable actions willed and planned in humans to a God Who is Wisdom itself.

We believe in a transcendent God Who is neither confined nor limited in terms of time and space. In His Immensity, God is beyond all limitations of place. And as we read in the Book of Wisdom, God's Spirit contains all things. "For the spirit of the Lord fills the world, is all-embracing, and knows what man says" (Wis 1:7).

Finally, one of the questions that seems to engage us over the centuries is what does God look like? We turn to the Book of Genesis for our answer: "God created man in His image, in the divine image He created him; male and female He created them" (Gn 1:27).

"Creator of Heaven and Earth"

279-314 **God's Beloved Creatures**

IN faith, we believe that God created the heavens and the earth and peopled the earth with very special human beings. God did not leave us on our own but favored His people with many kindnesses and provisions. Created in God's image, we, through faith, are aware that we are loved and gifted by God, and we appreciate the many gifts and privileges God gives His people. These gifts we call grace or graces.

Journeying toward God   293, 302

As Catholics, we believe that God has created us for Himself and that our major reason for being, or our goal in life, is personal union with God in His total presence in heaven. At the same time, as we journey toward God we believe and we are convinced that we can achieve our goal only through the help and assistance of God.

Furthermore, we are positive of God's substantial help. For we readily observe how, through the knowledge and love we experience as a characteristic of God's very nature, we can easily perceive that of all God's creatures we have been graced in a very special way. All this we know through faith.

The mystery of why God loves us in such a special and graced way is echoed in Paul's Letter to the Romans (5:5): "And hope does not disappoint, because the love of God has been poured out into our hearts through the Holy Spirit Who has been given to us."

Union with God   302, 51

Still, human life as we know and live it becomes a series of actions on an individual basis that can at times seemingly require heroic efforts. We can only grow and develop through the use of our faculties, especially mind and intellect. Certainly we acknowledge these powers as God's gifts. Moreover, in our struggle to grow, we see a need for acts of love, faith, and regret in our attempts to come even closer to God.

The beauty of this giving relationship is that the activities our individual efforts express are all graces accorded us by a loving God. We try to respond to the demands of the Gospel, and we resolve over and over again to live a positive life aimed toward union with God. We move toward the eternal reward promised. We cannot merit or work to achieve these graces. Rather God freely confers and cultivates His desire to have us work toward them.

307, 1730 Human Freedom and Christian Solidarity

Yet it is true that as human beings we are free to say no to the universal call to salvation that reflects God's will in our regard. Flooded with grace though we may be, we are not forced by God to respond to Him. We may reject the good that is presented to us. As the people of God, however, we support and encourage one another in a positive response to God's invitation to salvation, to His graces that are more than enough for us.

What is more, the people of God on earth carefully record, celebrate, and commemorate the lives and actions of sisters and brothers in Christ who have gone before us, who have been taken into the mystery of God's beatific presence. Our Saints are our treasured models of faith and grace. They are our hope for a mysterious promise given and totally accepted.

"And in Jesus Christ"

422, 464, 470 True God and True Man

WE believe that Jesus Christ is truly the Son of God Who became man for our benefit. There is almost universal acknowledgment that human beings are composed of body and soul. We believe that Jesus always had a Divine nature. At His conception and later birth in Bethlehem, Jesus was born a human being, with a human body and soul. Still, Jesus did not, given His human nature, cease to be God.

Hence, we acknowledge Jesus as God-Man, true God and true man. His human and Divine natures are inseparable in one Person Whom, in faith, we call Son of God.

In Paul's Letter to the Hebrews (1:1-4) we read: "In times past, God spoke in fragmentary and varied ways to our ancestors through the Prophets; in these last days, he has spoken to us through a Son, Whom He made heir of all things and through Whom He created the universe."

This Son "is the reflection of His glory, the very imprint of His being, and [He] sustains all things by His mighty word. When He had accomplished purification from sins, He took His seat at the right hand of the Majesty on high, as far superior to the angels as the name He has inherited is superior to theirs."

In the *Pastoral Constitution on the Church in the Modern World*, the Fathers of the Second Vatican Council reminded us that human nature was not set aside because Jesus Christ assumed it, but it has by that very fact been elevated to a Divine dignity. "For by His incarnation the Son of God has united Himself in some fashion with every human being (no. 22)."

Jesus used human hands at labor, thought with a human mind, acted by human choice, and loved His parents and friends with a human heart. "He has truly been made one of us, like us in all things except sin" *(Ibid).*

The Reign of God   422, 425

Jesus' baptism is the beginning of His public ministry. John baptized Jesus in terms of repentance. John anticipated the Kingdom, while Jesus through His miracles, healings, exorcisms, parables, and proclamations brings the Kingdom into His ministry.

The thrust of Jesus' message was the approaching nearness of the reign of God, a message He specifically directed to every segment of the population. In using "Abba" Jesus positions His role as that of a child in intimate relationship with its father. Jesus sees God as near to Himself and draws His followers into that close relationship.

Jesus' words and actions bespeak human traits of ignorance, anger, weariness, sorrow, joy, and social compassion. Jesus was certainly not an ascetic, and He and His disciples challenged the laws of cultic purity of His time. "The sabbath was made for man, not man for the sabbath" (Mk 2:27).

430-440 Jesus and Sinners

Jesus' public conduct was sometimes provocative—for example, when he ate and drank with sinners. In a highly selective and stratified society, Jesus kept "bad" company by associating with everybody; speaking to, blessing, healing, and feeding those segments of society considered ritually impure, the lepers particularly. His eating and drinking with sinners manifested the forgiveness of God.

At the same time, we must remember, Jesus was not a political revolutionary, since He clearly taught that the Kingdom of God does not come by violence or by human efforts. Jesus forgave sinners in healing since His mission was to proclaim the Kingdom to the lost sheep of Israel. "The spirit of the Lord is upon Me, because He has anointed Me to bring glad tidings to the poor" (Lk 4:18).

441-445 "His Only Son"

243, 249 Second Person of the Trinity

IN God there are three Persons: the Father, the Son, and the Holy Spirit, but these three Persons are only one God. That there are three Persons in God, we know only from Divine Revelation. It is a Mystery that remained hidden throughout Old Testament times but was revealed to us through Jesus.

When Jesus was baptized in the Jordan, all three Persons were in evidence. In the river stood the Son of God. From the heavens the Father's voice was heard, and the Holy Spirit descended in the form of a dove (Mt 3:16-17).

253-255 A Trinity of Persons

Any understanding of the Trinity has to begin with God the Father. God as a personal being is relational and seeks to share Himself. He knows Himself perfectly and speaks His word from all eternity, begetting God the Word, the perfect expression of the Father. One Divine essence exists in a double personhood, God knowing and God known.

Dialogue between the Father and the Word leads to the affirmation of perfect love or what we describe as the Holy Spirit. The Holy Spirit, as bond of love, is the inner connection between the Father and the Son, and as such, is the third Person.

There are four relations: (1) Father to Son; (2) Son to Father; (3) Son and Father to Holy Spirit; (4) Holy Spirit to Father and Son. To speak of "relation" here is a means to understand the uniqueness of each Person. Relationships arise out of action and reaction of each of the three Persons.

The three stand in dynamic tension with one another. Each Person is a subsistent relation. Thus, Father, Son, and Holy Spirit have to be explained simultaneously in God, three Persons, one nature. The Father is unbegotten, ungenerated; the Son is begotten but not created; and the Spirit proceeds from the Father and the Son.

Illustrations of the Trinity   253

We shall never be able to grasp the Mystery that is the Trinity; we can only believe it. Illustrations might help, but they do not explain the Mystery. For example, the illustration of three burning candles might help. Held close together, the three flames remain three. Join the three wicks and there is only one flame, but three candles.

St. Augustine spoke of one mind penetrated by three dimensions: (1) memory—Father; (2) understanding—Son; (3) love—Spirit. Irenaeus suggested a man with two hands; Son is left and Spirit is right.

Still, the Trinity remains a Mystery. Every time we make the sign of the cross we proclaim our faith in the Trinity, while voicing our hope of eventually entering fully into that great Mystery.

446-451

"Our Lord"

461-463 ## The Incarnation

THE Mystery of the Trinity enters our lives in the Incarnation. The "My Lord and my God" of the Apostle Thomas encompasses a long tradition of the Church that the specific purpose of the Incarnation was redemption for all people. The God-Man descended to earth for us that we might be redeemed in Christ and inherit eternal salvation in the full presence of the Trinity.

As Catholics, we believe in salvation. God the Father sent His Son to earth for this very purpose. In the life of Jesus His human response was obedience to the will of the Father. And the death, exaltation, Resurrection, and Ascension of the Son to the Father accomplished the pouring forth of the Holy Spirit, a Pentecost for all humanity.

436-440 ## Christ the Messiah and Redeemer

The distinction between early Christians and other Jewish peoples was that the former accepted Jesus as the Messiah, or the Christ. This same focus for the modern Christian is as true today as it was then. Looking back, we see that the early Church Fathers staunchly supported the redemptive character of the Incarnation, proclaiming that if Adam had not sinned, Christ would not have come to earth. St. Anselm also stressed the necessity of the Incarnation.

St. Thomas Aquinas did not totally agree, noting that God could have restored humankind absolutely without having sent His Son to suffer and die. Nonetheless, both sides of the question have carefully preserved the two essential elements of Incarnational traditions, namely, that Christ came into the world to redeem humanity and that Christ is the head and center of all creation.

It is indeed Christ on Calvary and the risen Christ in the Garden Who possesses primacy. The happy fault that has given humankind the sign of the cross is primary in Scripture and Tradition. The contrast between the first Adam and the Second Adam, Jesus Christ, rests in the filial act of obedience that placed Jesus on the Cross and led to His Resurrection and dominion over all humankind.

Salvation in Christ   541-546

With salvation accomplished, there comes that most signifi-cant relationship between God and His people. The shackles of the past slavery of sin have been unlinked, and all people are now called to, capable of, and given grace for an obedient response to the invitation to salvation. Fidelity to God is called for in the present in both general and individual response. God's fulsome reply is that He will always be available to serve His people.

Jesus died for all and Heaven is now thus open to all. It is up to God's people to accept, as Jesus did, the love and obedi-ence required for full membership in the Kingdom.

"Who Was Conceived by the Holy Spirit"   484-486

Spirit of Love and Power   689-702

WE see in the Christ-event a complex reality of many elements, including His Resurrection, death, life, and teachings, birth and baptism, Incarnation, Ascen-sion, and sending of the Holy Spirit. The Holy Spirit de-scended upon the Apostles on the day of Pentecost, in the form of fiery tongues.

The Holy Spirit had been active in just souls of the past and also in the Apostles before the Pentecost event, but on that day He came bringing the fullness of His grace and gifts. The Holy Spirit (1) sanctified the Apostles; (2) enlightened them so that they understood the teaching of Jesus clearly and correctly; (3) strengthened them so that they preached without fear; (4) and bestowed on them the gifts of tongues and working miracles.

The Spirit's Presence on the Apostles

A T the miracle of Pentecost, the prophetic words of John the Baptist were fulfilled: "One mightier than I is coming.... He will baptize you with the Holy Spirit and fire" (Lk 3:16).

In the *Dogmatic Constitution on the Church,* Vatican II explains: "The Lord Jesus ... sent [the Apostles] first to the children of Israel and then to all nations, so that as sharers in His power they might make all people His disciples, and sanctify and govern them, and thus spread His Church, and by ministering to it under the guidance of the Lord, direct it all days even to the consummation of the world" (no. 19).

Fully confirmed in their mission on Pentecost day, the Apostles experienced the fulfillment of Jesus' promise: "You will receive power when the Holy Spirit comes upon you, and you will be My witnesses in Jerusalem, throughout Judea and Samaria, and to the ends of the earth" (Acts 1:8).

The Spirit's Presence Today

Today Bishops and all minister-helpers serve the Christian community "presiding in place of God" over His people. Their authority is grounded in the Holy Spirit. What the Spirit authorizes is what the community of servants, namely the Church, accomplishes. God revealing and God inspiring cannot be separated.

Through proclamation, worship, the Sacraments, service, witness, and an ongoing spiritual growth we see, understand, and believe in the ever present activity of the Holy Spirit in the Church and its shepherds.

"Born of the Virgin Mary"

Mother of God

C ATHOLICS believe that the Blessed Virgin Mary is the Mother of Jesus, the God-Man, and thus we likewise call Mary the Mother of God. The archangel Gabriel announced to Mary that she had been chosen to be the Mother of God. When Mary objected that she was not married, the angel told her: "The Holy Spirit will come upon you, and the power of the Most High will overshadow you. Therefore the child to be born will be called holy, Son of God. . . ." Mary's obedient response was: "I am the handmaid of the Lord. May it be done to me according to your word" (Lk 1:30-38).

Mother and Associate of the Redeemer   502-507

In the Second Vatican Council's *Dogmatic Constitution on the Church* we read: "Predestined from eternity, by that decree of divine providence which determined the incarnation of the Word, to be the Mother of God, the Blessed Virgin was on this earth the virgin Mother of the Redeemer, and above all others and in a singular way the generous associate and humble handmaid of the Lord. She conceived, brought forth, and nourished Christ; she presented Him to the Father in the Temple, and was united with Him by compassion as He died on the Cross. . . .

"By her belief and obedience, not knowing man but overshadowed by the Holy Spirit, as the new Eve she brought forth on earth the very Son of the Father, showing an undefiled faith, not in the word of the ancient serpent, but in that of God's messenger" (nos. 61, 63).

Marian Acts of Piety   971-972

From the earliest times of the Church, we have honored the Blessed Virgin. Various forms of piety as regards Mary, approved by the Church, have developed over time. In all this, where the Mother of God is honored, the Son is correctly glorified.

Moreover, the Church urges the frequent practice of all approved devotions and acts of piety toward the Blessed Virgin, especially those exercised within the liturgy. At the same time, the Church reminds us that all devotion to Mary proceeds from a true and stable faith, one that leads to a knowledge of Mary's virtues and to their imitation.

971 Characteristics of Marian Devotions

In his Apostolic Exhortation on *Devotion to the Blessed Virgin Mary* issued in 1974, Pope Paul VI spoke of authentic veneration of Mary. Moreover, he called for greater use of the Rosary and the Litany of the Blessed Virgin. Further, he listed four characteristics of Marian devotions in our time:

(1) They must be rooted in the Bible. Prayers and chants connected with Mary should be inspired by and worded according to the Bible, while taking care that these be infused with significant themes of Christianity.

(2) They must be harmonized with the liturgy and not merged into it.

(3) They must be ecumenical in character, avoiding any kind of exaggeration that would mislead other Christian sisters and brothers about the true teaching of the Church.

(4) They must be in harmony with modern anthropological studies, paying close attention to the findings of the human sciences.

Generally speaking, Pope Paul VI reiterated what has always been the mind of the Church, that, abuses aside, veneration of Mary does not detract from Christ, but points to Him and redounds to His glory.

571-628

"Suffered under Pontius Pilate, was Crucified, Died and Was Buried"

571, 595, 599, 613, 624
Scripture and Tradition

IN this article of our Creed we see specific events in the Life of Jesus. We become more intensely aware of Jesus' passage through human history. The historical character, Pontius Pilate, is here named. His place in secular history is without question. Moreover, the Son of God suffers death for the sins of all people at a specific time in history, notably during Pilate's reign. This redemptive event within the context of time as we know it, is a significant segment of the Church's Tradition.

For Catholics there is a Sacred Tradition that is the Word of God given to the Apostles by Christ and the Holy Spirit and handed down to their successors. The Church teaches these by means of prayer and creeds, liturgical practices, and authoritative writings. Tradition is the way the Church understands and lives the teachings of Jesus at any given moment in time. Moreover, Sacred Scripture and Tradition form one body of God's Word. This segment of knowledge, guarded by the Church, becomes the paramount source of revelation for humanity.

Founded on the Cross   616, 662

We see in this article our belief that the starting point of Christian existence and the core of the New Testament message is the theology of the Cross, wherein our God does not wait until we sinners go to be reconciled, but rather He comes to meet us and forgive us. The Cross explains the necessity of our being totally receptive to God's preferred reconciliation, while, at the same time, letting ourselves be totally taken over by Him, letting God act on us.

Living Our Faith   142-165

The beauty of both Scripture and Tradition is that they serve as guides for what we are to believe as we reply to God's invitation to salvation. Scripture is the written word of God inspired by the Holy Spirit. To the Apostles and their successors Tradition passes on in full purity the word of God. Favored by the light of the Holy Spirit, the successors of the Apostles preach, explain, circulate, and preserve the truth of God's word.

In First Corinthians 12:2-6 we read: "You know how, when you were pagans, you were constantly attracted and led away to mute idols. Therefore, I tell you that nobody speaking by the Spirit of God says, 'Jesus be accursed.' And no one can say, 'Jesus is Lord,' except by the Holy Spirit. There are different kinds of spiritual gifts but the same Spirit; there are different forms of service but the same Lord; there are different workings but the same God Who produces all of them in everyone."

We see then that God's people are free to grow through study and contemplation; through preachings and understandings of those who proclaim the truth. Hence the possibility for growth in understanding our essential beliefs through qualified expression marked with greater clarity or development, and conveyed through the Magisterium of the Church.

In living what we believe as a community of God's people we celebrate Eucharist, our essential form of worship in thanksgiving. Actions to build the body of the Church and serve the needs of the poor flow from our worship. In addition, achievements in poetry, the visual arts, literature, music, architecture, philosophy, and scientific advances further reflect the truths we as a community glean from Scripture and Tradition. (See *National Catechetical Directory*, no. 59.)

631-658 ## "He Descended into Hell and on the Third Day He Rose from the Dead"

632-635 ### The Threat of Death

WHEN we speak of our Lord's descent into hell we are struck with a sense of mysteriousness. Jesus becomes obscure in death as we contemplate the cold nights of the tomb. There is only a deep and penetrating silence there. It is a silence that speaks to us and, indeed, according to Cardinal Ratzinger, becomes a part of revelation.

He speaks of "silence, inaccessible, uncomprehended and incomprehensible," a facet of the Son of God that eludes us. We come to know the radical loneliness that Jesus experienced in the Garden and on the Cross. "In truth one thing is certain, there exists a night into whose solitude no voice reaches; there is a door through which we can only walk alone—the door of death. Death is absolute loneliness. But the loneliness into which love can no longer reach is hell."

Jesus' Resurrection Brings Life

638, 647,
651-654

Jesus, Who came that all might have life forever, valued love for all of us more than His life. That very love is thus the source of His immortality and the immortality He holds out to His people. Thus, we believe that on the third day after His death Jesus reunited His soul and body and rose in glory from the grave.

The Resurrection of Jesus is the greatest and most significant event of our Catholic Faith. We stand with St. Paul when he states: "If Christ has not been raised, then empty too is our preaching; empty, too, is your faith" (1 Cor 15:14).

Testimony of the Apostles about the Resurrection

639-642

This Resurrection of Jesus is one segment of our Faith that is constantly being challenged. And so we must confront ourselves with the question: how do we know Christ rose from the dead? We turn to the testimony of the Apostles. They saw the risen Jesus. They spoke with Him and touched Him. Finally, they gave their lives for Him. This testimony is frequently dismissed as having been a figment of the Apostles' minds.

Admittedly there are differences in the Gospels about the event and Jesus' post-Resurrection appearances. Still, all the Gospels agree that Jesus rose from the dead and made several appearances. The variety in detail gives every evidence that the Apostles did not get together to concoct an identical story.

No one actually saw Jesus rise. The empty tomb, the post-Resurrection appearances, and the willingness of the Apostles to preach Christ risen at the risk of death that eventually took them all, is a very strong indicator. Moreover, the history of that day down to our time has produced no evidence of a conspiracy.

Jesus' Resurrection confirms our faith in Jesus as the Son of God and gives us hope that sometime we too shall be raised from death. "Destroy this temple and in three days I will raise it up" (Jn 2:19). "Just as in Adam all die, so too in Christ shall all be brought to life" (1 Cor 15:22).

659-664   ## "He Ascended into Heaven and Sits at the Right Hand of the Father"

659   ### Meaning of Jesus' Ascension

WHEN we say that Jesus ascended into heaven, we proclaim a truth that reflects many aspects of our Faith. In no sense of the term do we consider this to be a journey into outer space. Rather the Ascension reflects the destiny of Jesus so clearly projected in revelation, while, at the same time, it reminds us of the spiritual and moral response we are called to make by living the truths of the Gospel, so that we might also share Jesus' destiny.

The Ascension means the attainment of a fulness of life, specifically a life that is essentially different from all earthly life of our experience insofar as it is freed from the limitations of the forms of existence familiar to us.

While it is true that the number "forty days" would leave a mathematical plus or minus, it is really more symbolic than literal. In Acts 1:3, we read: "He presented Himself alive to [the Apostles] by many proofs after He had suffered, appearing to them during forty days and speaking about the kingdom of God." In a sense, the author records the last of Jesus' visible appearances to the Apostles.

663   ### Union with God

In faith then, we believe Jesus was reunited with the Father in a special way; ". . . and sits at the right hand of the Father." Even as man, Jesus participates in the power and glory of our Father in heaven. But, "God is not the prisoner of His eternity. In Jesus He has time for us, and Jesus is this in actual fact 'the throne of grace' to which at any time we can 'draw near with confidence' " (Ratzinger). When Jesus is with us, He is in time, and when He is with God He is in eternity.

As Paul reminds us, "Seek what is above, where Christ is seated at the right hand of God" (Col 3:1). For the followers of

Christ the ways to live following His Ascension are outlined in Paul's exhortation to the Philippians: "Have among yourselves the same attitude that is also yours in Christ, Who, though He was in the form of God . . . emptied Himself, and taking the form of a slave, coming in human likeness; . . . Because of this, God greatly exalted Him and bestowed on Him the name that is above every name, that at the name of Jesus every knee should bend . . . and every tongue confess Jesus Christ is Lord, to the glory of God the Father" (Phil 2:5-11).

"From Thence He Will Come Again to Judge the Living and the Dead" 668-686

Judgment 668, 678

WE Catholics believe Jesus will come again at the end of the world to judge all people and bring Redemption to final fulfillment. This judgment is called the General Judgment. Naturally, we will be held accountable for any sin that may have been part of our lives. Like the sin of Adam and Eve, when we knowingly and deliberately break one of God's commands or laws, we commit sin.

We, in reality, disobey God through an inner act of disrespect, perhaps motivated by opposition to limits set down by God's commandments, or a disbelief that God truly loves us, or an overwhelming desire for the person, place, thing, or action that, in freedom, we fully embrace. Moreover, we know that some of the sinful actions we perform, fisticuffs, for example, can do us physical harm, while, at the same time, rupturing our relationship with God. We then become accountable for our actions/sins.

The Christian Attitude 673, 675

The reality of our responsibility is reflected in the *Dogmatic Constitution on the Church*, wherein Vatican II comments: "Since we know not the day nor the hour, on our Lord's advice we must be constantly vigilant. Thus, when we have finished the course of our earthly life, we may merit to enter into the marriage feast with Him and to be numbered among the blessed. Thus we may not be ordered to go into eternal fire like the wicked and slothful servant, into the exterior darkness where there will be the weeping and the gnashing of teeth.

"For before we reign with Christ in glory, all of us will be made manifest before the tribunal of Christ, so that each one may receive his or her recompense, good or bad, according to his or her life in the body. Then at the end of the world they who have done right shall rise to life; the evildoers shall rise to be damned.

"We reckon, therefore, that the sufferings of this present time are as nothing compared with the glory to be revealed in us. Strong in faith, we await . . . the appearing of the glory of the great God and Savior Christ Jesus, Who will give a new form to this lowly body of ours and remake it according to the pattern of His glorified body and Who will come to be glorified in His holy ones and adored by all who have believed" (no. 48).

679 A Merciful Judge

But, as Cardinal Ratzinger notes, our credal statement on the judgment must be understood in the context of Jesus' message of mercy: "It is not simply . . . God, the Infinite, the Unknown, the Eternal Who judges. . . . He has handed the judgment over to the One Who, as man, is our brother."

683-741
"I Believe in the Holy Spirit"

737 The Sanctifier

WE believe that the Holy Spirit dwells in the Church, in its leadership and in its people. Principally, the work of the Holy Spirit within the Church is the sanctification of its members. As we saw above, the Holy Spirit on Pentecost day brought the fullness of His grace and gifts to the Church.

Today these gifts are preserved not only through the preaching and teaching of the successors to the Apostles but also in our individual lives. At Baptism we receive the Holy Spirit, and in Confirmation we open ourselves to a more mature acceptance and recognition of the Holy Spirit dwelling within us.

Divine Indwelling   739-741

The notion of the Holy Spirit being personally present to each of us is referred to as the Divine Indwelling. Although we people of the world are rich in diversity, for those who follow Jesus in the Church the title "Catholic" bespeaks the presence of the Holy Spirit, and an ongoing viable unity from the Bishops to the Pope, and to every other believer without exception.

This sanctifying indwelling of the Holy Spirit enables God's people to respond fully to His call to eternal life. It is important that, given our awareness of the Divine Indwelling, we live our lives in a growing acknowledgment of the presence of God not only in ourselves but also in every other person. "I shall walk before the Lord in the land of the living" (Ps 116:9).

As Thomas Merton reminded us, the world is not just a physical space traversed by jet planes and filled with people running in all directions. It is a complex of responsibilities and options, stemming from the loves, hates, fears, joys, hopes, greed, cruelty, kindness, faith, trust, and suspicion of all human beings.

If we are determined to live our lives in the conscious awareness of the Holy Spirit dwelling within us, we know, in hope, we can make a better place of the world. Lives of virtue are indeed possible through the Holy Spirit.

The Theological Virtues   1812

As we grow, therefore, in Christian holiness, we try to live out the implications of the *theological virtues* of faith, hope, and charity, which are infused in the soul by God and are a source of sanctifying grace. "The love of God has been poured out into our hearts through the Holy Spirit Who has been given to us" (Rom 5:5). "So faith, hope, love remain, these three; but the greatest of these is love" (1 Cor 13:13).

1805 **The Moral Virtues**

There are other virtues known as the *moral virtues*. These tend to regulate our lives in a manner both acceptable and pleasing to God. The four cardinal virtues—so named because all other moral virtues hinge on them, are contained in them, and flow from them—are prudence, temperance, justice, and fortitude.

Prudence allows us to do good actions in light of our spiritual welfare and salvation. We gain control over our passions and evil desires through *temperance*. Our sense of *justice* encourages us to see all people as equal and to act toward all as temples of the Holy Spirit. Finally, when we must choose between right and wrong, when we are subjected to temptation, *fortitude* helps us make the right decisions and rise to overcome challenges and meet opposition to our faith.

748-983

"The Holy Catholic Church, the Communion of Saints"

1076,
1113,
1210 **The Sacraments**

WHEN Catholics celebrate the Sacraments we believe we experience the life of the Spirit that has energized the Church from its beginnings in Apostolic times. Through the life of grace conferred in the Sacraments our one Faith spans the ages.

Our disposition in celebrating the Sacraments should reflect our conviction that we have received the Sacraments through the Apostles from Jesus Christ. Given this sacred Tradition, the Sacraments need no redefinition or new purposes. Their significance rests solely on the fact that through life-giving elements they are the Lord's gifts to us, His life-conferring actions upon us. Hence we celebrate the Lord's actions in our regard with profound respect, dignity, and great joy in the knowledge of His abiding presence with us in a special way in His Sacraments.

Christ instituted seven Sacraments or outward signs that give grace. Sacramental signs, like water or oil for example, point to and bring the grace of the Sacraments. These outward signs were created to teach us humbly to submit to material things or means through which we receive spiritual graces. Vatican II in its *Dogmatic Constitution on the Church* reminds us: "In that Body [the Church] the life of Christ is poured into believers, who, through the Sacraments are united in a hidden and real way to Christ Who suffered and was glorified" (no. 7).

In the *Constitution on the Sacred Liturgy* we note: "The purpose of the Sacraments is to sanctify human beings . . . and . . . to give worship to God; because they are signs, they also instruct . . . they do indeed impart grace, but, in addition, the very act of celebrating them most effectively disposes the faithful to receive this grace in a fruitful manner, to worship God duly, and to practice charity." Thus it is important for the faithful to frequent the Sacraments (no 59).

Although there are seven Sacraments, here we treat only six, since we will discuss Reconciliation below. The six are as follows:

Baptism

1213-1274

Through Baptism we are incorporated into Christ. We are buried with Christ, and out of that comes new life through Christ's Resurrection. Christ impregnates the waters of Baptism with His risen life. The white garment is a sign of new life, in which the baptized are freed from Satan or slavery. Baptism is the most necessary Sacrament because without Baptism no one can be saved. "Go into the whole world and proclaim the Good News to every creature. Whoever believes and is baptized will be saved; whoever does not believe will be condemned" (Mk 16:15-16). Finally, Baptism takes away original sin, all personal sin, and all punishment due to sin and confers sanctifying grace.

Confirmation

1285-1314

Confirmation is the Sacrament in which the Christian is strengthened for the mature practice and profession of faith.

In Baptism we become members of the Faith; in Confirmation we become witnessing members. We are empowered to speak or act for God. Through Confirmation we are identified as servants and soldiers of Christ. The fullness of the Holy Spirit helps us to remain true to our Faith; sanctifying grace is increased; and we become more intimately connected with Holy Eucharist.

1322-1419 Holy Eucharist *(See also pp. 39-46)*

Holy Eucharist is a Sacrament in which Christ Himself is truly though not visibly present as God and Man, with His glorified Body and Blood, under the appearances of bread and wine, to offer Himself on the altar as our sacrifice and to give Himself as our sacrificial food.

"The Eucharistic celebration is a holy meal which recalls the Last Supper, reminds us of our unity with one another in Christ, and anticipates the banquet of the kingdom. In the Eucharist, Christ the Lord nourishes Christians, not only with His word but especially with His Body and Blood, effecting a transformation which impels them toward greater love of God and neighbor" *(National Catechetical Directory,* no. 120).

Jesus promised the Holy Eucharist in the words: "The bread that I will give is My flesh for the life of the world. The Jewish people quarreled among themselves, saying, 'How can this man give us His flesh to eat?' Jesus said to them, 'Amen, amen, I say to you, unless you eat the flesh of the Son of Man and drink His blood, you do not have life within you. Whoever eats My flesh and drinks My blood has eternal life, and I will raise him on the last day. For My flesh is true food, and My blood is true drink'" (Jn 6:51-55).

Jesus instituted the Holy Eucharist on the night before He suffered and died. When Jesus spoke the words "This is My Body, this is My Blood" (see Mt 26:26-28), He changed the bread into His sacred Body and the wine into His precious Blood. With the words: "Do this in memory of Me" (see Lk 22:19), Jesus conferred upon the Apostles the power also to change bread into His sacred Body and wine into His precious Blood. His power to change bread and wine was handed on to bishops and priests.

That Jesus is truly present in the Holy Eucharist we know: from the words by which Jesus promised and instituted the Sacrament; and from the teaching of the Apostle Paul and the Church.

The Sacrifice of the New Covenant is the Sacrifice of Jesus Christ on the Cross, which becomes present in an unbloody manner in the Sacrifice of the Mass (the Eucharist). The Holy Sacrifice of the Mass is the perpetual unbloody sacrifice of the New Covenant in which the Sacrifice of the Cross is made sacramentally yet truly present.

Anointing of the Sick

1499-
1532

The Sacrament of the Anointing of the Sick is for Christians who are seriously ill as a result of sickness or old age. Through the Sacrament of Anointing Christ strengthens the faithful who are afflicted with illness, providing them with the strongest means of support.

There are three distinct parts in celebrating this Sacrament: (a) *the prayer of faith,* in which the people pray in faith for the sick, initiating the presence of the whole Church; (b) *the laying on of hands,* a gesture by the priest through which is indicated that the individual is the object of the Church's prayer of faith; and (c) *the anointing with oil,* which is a symbol of healing. The priest prays: "Through this holy anointing may the Lord in His love and mercy help you with the grace of the Holy Spirit. May the Lord Who frees you from sin save you and raise you up."

Holy Orders

1536-
1600

Holy Orders is the Sacrament by which the office of bishop, priest, or deacon, together with its power and grace, is conferred. The outward sign of Holy Orders is the laying on of the hands and the simultaneous prayer of the bishop. Both Scripture and Tradition attest to Jesus' having instituted Holy Orders.

The Sacrament, in addition to spiritually marking the priest, bestows the powers of the priesthood, increases sanctifying grace, and strengthens the priest for his mission.

1601-
1666
Marriage

God instituted Marriage in paradise, and Christ raised it to a Sacrament. In this Sacrament, Christ joins man and woman in a holy and indissoluble union and enables them to share in the mystery of the love between Christ and His Church by conferring graces to fulfill their roles as husband, wife, and parents.

In addition to sanctifying grace, Marriage gives that special grace needed to remain faithful to the duties of the married state. Married people are expected to live in love till death; help one another lead good Catholic lives; and teach their offspring about God and His special love, care, and concern for them.

As members of the Church, and participants in the Sacraments, Catholics believe they are in close union with one another, with the souls in purgatory and the Saints in heaven. In the *Dogmatic Constitution on the Church,* Vatican II states, "Until the Lord shall come in His majesty . . . some of His disciples are exiles on earth, some having died are being purified and others are in glory . . . but all in various ways and degrees are in communion in the same charity of God and neighbor. . . . For all who are in Christ, having His Spirit, form one Church and cleave together in Him..." (nos. 49, 51).

976-987
"The Forgiveness of Sins"

1422,
1440-
1445
Reconciliation with God and the Church

CATHOLICS believe that the Sacrament of Penance, also called Reconciliation, was instituted by Jesus when He gave the Apostles and their successors the power to forgive sins. When, after Baptism, we commit sin we may through this Sacrament be reconciled with God and gain reentry into the state of grace.

Jesus constantly urged His listeners to conversion of life. The Church continues to do the same to this very moment. Since sin affects not only ourselves but also the entire Church, when we participate in the Sacrament of Penance we are reconciled both to

God and to all God's people. We obtain mercy and pardon from God for our sins. For this reason we make every effort to be completely and totally converted to God.

Rite of Reconciliation   1446-60

The Sacrament of Reconciliation entails a threefold process: (1) contrition and confession; (2) satisfaction; and (3) absolution.

Naturally, contrition is most important wherein we develop a true sorrow and hatred for our sins on the one hand, and a sincere determination never again to sin.

Then we literally confess, speak or divulge our sins to a duly authorized priest. We speak what we truly believe the condition of our soul to be, or what our conscience informs us is offensive in the mind of God. Given our conversion of heart we then willingly perform some duty/action as a form of reparation or satisfaction for the sins we have committed and confessed. We literally change our life-style or make amends to all who have been offended by our sin.

Finally, through a visible sign that we call absolution, the priest speaks the formula of absolution while, at the same time, making the Sign of the Cross over the penitent. Through this action, God pardons the sins confessed to the priest confessor.

It is most important to remember that Catholics believe that God alone forgives sins. The priest or confessor is merely God's instrument through whom God exercises His loving mercy and forgiveness.

Ongoing Penance   1434-
                                                             1439
Although we experience Christ in the Sacrament of Reconciliation, we have a tendency to go back to sin. We are constantly on the road to conversion. Moreover, there are human dimensions of the Church that are in need of conversion. And this conversion process is due to the ever present divine initiation in the Church. That is why conversion and repentance are so essential within the Church.

Pope Paul VI reminded the Church that prayer, fasting, and almsgiving are signs of the ongoing conversion process. Moreover, penitential acts and activities are not degrading, their purpose being to reaffirm the holiness and mystery of God. At the same time, penance aims at the liberation of God's people. The Sacrament of Reconciliation frees God's people to become closer and closer to the reality that was Christ in His public ministry, namely, living, preaching, and teaching forgiveness of sins.

998-1060

"The Resurrection of the Body and Life Everlasting"

992 Fullness of Life after Death

HERE we see summed up in one phrase the totality of the object of Christian hope. Through our cooperation and response to the Holy Spirit we live in hope of sharing in the promise of the plenitude of life after death. In this condition we will participate in the very life of God, particularly that intrinsic quality of the life of God that is eternity.

1023-
1029 The Beatific Vision

Theologically we use the term Beatific Vision by which we mean that we experience God face to face. Once this happens we will be completely satisfied, absolutely fulfilled, never again to experience desires, disappointments, needs, or cares. Our joy, happiness, and spiritual growth and development will be totally complete. Nothing more could possibly be added. The Beatific Vision transcends every possible human or historical experience.

In the Book of Revelation we read: "Nothing unclean will enter it [heaven]" (21:27). Vatican II in its *Dogmatic Constitution on the Church,* (no. 49) expresses the Catholic teaching that those in heaven, in glory, behold God Himself triune and one, as He is.

In a general audience on May 22, 1974, Pope Paul VI said: "We now live in time, but one day we shall live forever in the Kingdom of heaven. This does not mean the blue sky above but the new state of existence produced in a mysterious and wonderful manner according to God's creative plan and by His power. It is a Kingdom in which we share even now in virtue of certain supernatural conditions and gifts like faith, grace, and divine love. We are partly of earth and partly of heaven. We must know how to live simultaneously on earth and in heaven."

A New World

1042-1050

And what of the material world? At the least, should it survive it would be transformed radically. According to Michael Schmauss, "Heaven . . . is nothing other than the future glorified humanity on a glorified earth, or a glorified creation" *(Dogma* 6, p. 273). Everything in creation will, in its finality, glorify the Creator. "Eye has not seen nor has ear heard, nor has it entered in the human heart what God has prepared for those who love Him" (1 Cor 2:9).

The Blessed

1024-1025, 2030

Finally, it is important for us to understand that all who enter heaven comprise the Blessed not just the canonized Saints.

PART 2

POPULAR PRAYERS

Introduction

THE discovery of intimacy with God, the necessity for adoration, the need for intercession—the experience of Christian holiness shows us the fruitfulness of prayer, in which God reveals Himself to the spirit and hearts of His servants (Vatican II).

The very fabric of our belief(s) is interwoven with the idea and practice of prayer. Prayer can take many forms. For the Catholic the highest form of public prayer is the Holy Sacrifice of the Mass. The entire public prayer of the Universal Church centers around the Divine Liturgy.

There are innumerable ways in which to pray and many methods of prayer. One of the greatest helps to prayer for most people is a fixed series of prayers. It puts at our fingertips a precious treasury of words by which we can approach God every day. Such ready-made prayers imprint on our minds the sentiments that the Church wants us to have in prayer.

Prayers of this type also convey a deeper knowledge and understanding of the Church's teaching. In a subtle and unobtrusive fashion they teach the Faith while allowing us to approach God. By using them we not only get closer to God but also get to know Him better with every passing day.

It goes without saying that we can also pray in our words instead of words found on a printed page—and indeed we must do so. However, ready-made prayers are there for those times when we do not know what to say and need help in speaking to God. We need the help of past ages as well as present trends to say what we feel and what we should feel.

Contemplation or meditation follows as a significant life-giving and sustaining dialogue with God. In contemplation we become aware of our basic relationship with God. That is, we come to know, understand, enjoy, and appreciate God's sustaining presence in our lives. The realization that we live, breathe, move, and exist through God's presence in His creatures enables us to more fully ground our beliefs into a rhythm of life, a contemplative spirit that becomes second nature to us.

It is a wisdom expressed fully in the knowledge and joy that God is, and it is only because such is the truth that we are, we live, we exist. This intimacy with God enables us to live our lives in such a fashion that prayer-contemplation becomes a source of strength, happiness, courage, and peace. It is salvation already underway.

This is not to say that we do not carry our humanity any longer; not at all. Given our human nature, one that Christ shared during His life on earth, we are aware of personal failings, needs of the Church and community, longings to speak to God in words that express specific concerns. Frequently called intercessory prayer, it may take many forms and address many issues.

There are also a number of sentiments with which we should pray. We must pray with (1) *devotion*, i.e., we speak from the heart, avoiding distractions as much as possible; (2) *humility*, i.e., we acknowledge our sinfulness and need for help; (3) *resignation*, i.e., we leave it to God's will as to whether and how he will hear us; (4) *confidence*, i.e., we trust that God will hear us; and (5) *perseverance*, i.e., we continue to pray even though our prayer is not heard at once or as soon as we would like.

We present here a number of prayers that are in common usage, while others are concerned with special categories one might want to address in God's presence. They are preceded by a short explanation of the Mass—our greatest prayer.

At the Last Supper, Jesus said: "Do this as a remembrance of me

THE MASS—OUR GREATEST PRAYER

1341-
1390 AT the Last Supper, on the night when He was betrayed, our Savior instituted the Eucharistic sacrifice of His Body and Blood. He did this in order to perpetuate the sacrifice of the Cross throughout the centuries until He should come again.

Thus the Mass is:

1) the *true sacrifice* of the New Covenant, in which a holy and living Victim is offered, Jesus Christ, and we in union with Him, as a gift of love and obedience to the Father;

2) a *sacred meal* and *spiritual banquet* of the children of God;

3) a *Paschal meal*, which evokes the passage (passover) of Jesus from this world to the Father; it renders Him present and makes Him live again in souls, and it anticipates our definitive passage to the Kingdom of God;

4) a *communitarian meal*, that is, a gathering together of the Head and His members, of Jesus and His Church, His Mystical Body, in order to carry out a perfect divine worship.

Thus, the Mass is the greatest prayer we have. Through it we give thanks and praise to the Father for the wonderful future He has given us in His Son. We also ask forgiveness for our sins and beg the Father's blessing upon ourselves and our fellow human beings all over the world.

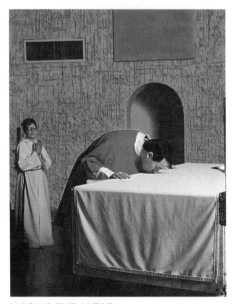

KISSING THE ALTAR

INTRODUCTORY RITES

THE Eucharist consists of the Liturgy of the Word and the Liturgy of the Eucharist plus introductory and concluding rites.

During the Introductory Rites acts of prayer and penitence prepare us to meet Christ as He comes in Word and Sacrament. We gather as a worshiping community to celebrate our unity with and in Him.

Beginning of Mass

AS a sign of adoration, the celebrant kisses the altar, which represents Christ. Then he greets the people—thus connecting both parties of the Eucharistic dialogue: God and us. At the same time the Entrance Song or Antiphon provides us with the theme of the day.

The Opening Prayer

WE then ask to be purified before hearing God's Word and celebrating His Eucharist. Next we turn our attention to praise and thanksgiving: the Kyrie and Gloria.

In the Opening Prayer, the priest invites us to pray for a moment and then in our name petitions God the Father through the mediation of Christ in the Holy Spirit. We bring to our prayer our pains, our cares, the concerns of our family, friends, and the whole world. We then ratify the prayer with our Amen.

OPENING PRAYER

40

LITURGY OF THE WORD

THE proclamation of God's Word is always centered on Christ. Jesus is the Word of God Himself and the Author of Revelation. It is He Himself Who speaks to us when the Sacred Scriptures are liturgically proclaimed.

First and Second Readings

CHRIST is present through His Word as the Readings are proclaimed. The Old Testament writings prepare for Him, and the New Testament writings speak of Him directly.

In the Responsorial Psalm we reflect upon God's words and respond to them.

The Gospel

WE then rise out of respect to show our love and admiration for Jesus Who will speak to us in the Gospel. He comes to proclaim His Word (through the priest or deacon) to us here and now and to enable us to apply it to our lives today.

God's Word is spoken again in the Homily. The Holy Spirit speaking through the lips of the preacher explains and applies the day's biblical readings to the needs of a particular congregation. He calls us to respond to Christ through the life we lead.

41

FIRST READING

THE GOSPEL

THE PROFESSION OF FAITH

The Profession of Faith (Creed)

AFTER listening to God's Word, reflecting on it, and responding in our hearts to it, we now make a corporate profession of faith. We publicly respond, assent, and adhere to that Word. This is a response not only to doctrinal propositions but also to the person of Christ present in the Word

The Creed used is the Nicene Creed (although the Apostles' Creed may also be used at times, especially in children's Masses). This is a summary of the faith expressed by the Councils of Nicaea (325) and of Constantinople (381) as ratified by the Council of Chalcedon (451).

The General Intercessions

INSTRUCTED, moved and renewed by the Word of God that brought Christ into our midst, we are now ready to exercise our priestly function by interceding for all mankind. We pray for the needs of the Church and the world as well as the current needs of our local parish community.

The celebrant sets the stage for the prayer and sums it up at the end, and the reader articulates its petitions, but it is the assembly that makes the prayer by its invocation.

THE GENERAL INTERCESSIONS

LITURGY OF THE EUCHARIST

WE enter now into the Eucharistic sacrifice itself, the Supper of the Lord. We are God's new people, the redeemed brothers and sisters of Christ, gathered around his table.

Offering of the People's Gifts

THE people bring forward their gifts of bread and wine as well as their monetary offerings for the upkeep of the church building and the clergy, and the relief of the poor. These are but a symbol of their inner readiness to give God all of themselves with their hopes and disappointments, their work and leisure, and their whole everyday lives.

Preparation of the Gifts

THESE are prayers of blessing of God's goodness. We bless God for the gifts of bread and wine (food and drink), for He is the creator of all things. We also bless Him for giving us the power to collaborate with Him in bringing forth His gifts by our dedicated labor and applied intelligence.

Afterward, we pray that our sacrifice will benefit all and then assent to the priest's prayer in our name that God will bless and accept our gifts.

OFFERING OF THE PEOPLE'S GIFTS

PREPARATION OF THE GIFTS

CONSECRATION OF THE BREAD

CONSECRATION OF THE WINE

THE GREAT AMEN

The Eucharistic Prayer

THE Eucharistic service of praise and thanksgiving is the center of the celebration. We join Christ in His sacrifice, celebrating His memorial and acknowledging the wonderful works of God in our lives.

At the consecration of the bread and wine Christ's words spoken through the priest accomplish what they signify: His Eucharistic body and blood, His Real Presence with all the riches of the Kingdom.

The people now praise Christ in the Memorial Acclamation. We celebrate the fact that Christ has redeemed us, is with us now to apply that Redemption to each of us, and will return in glory to perfect that Redemption for all.

The Church then offers the Victim to the Father in the Holy Spirit.

The Great Amen

AT the end of the Eucharistic Prayer the priest offers praise and honor to the Father through Christ Who is the High Priest, with Christ Who is present in the sacrificial memorial, and in Christ Who gives Himself to His members.

The people endorse these sentiments by their Great Amen. It says that we have joined in praising the Father for all His wonderful works and have offered ourselves with Jesus to Him.

44

COMMUNION RITE

THE Communion Rite is the conclusion of the Mass. It is the part when God gives a gift to us after we have presented our gift to Him: Jesus Christ, the Son of God and Savior of the world.

The Our Father

THIS rite begins with the magnificent prayer left us by our Lord—the Our Father. In it we ask for our daily bread, the bread that gives access to eternity, the Bread of Life.

Communion of the Priest

AFTER prayers that stress brotherly love, the spirit of reconciliation, and the unity of Christians, the priest and people receive Communion. Communion is administered to the people via a procession accompanied by song. This expresses the real unity, spiritual joy, and brotherly love of those assembled to offer and communicate.

Communion of the People

THE minister of communion says: "The Body of Christ" and the communicant says: "Amen." We should ever bear in mind St. Cyprian's words: "It is not idly that you say Amen. You are professing that you receive the Body of Christ.... Thus, keep in your heart what you profess with your lips!"

45

THE OUR FATHER

COMMUNION OF THE PRIEST

COMMUNION OF THE PEOPLE

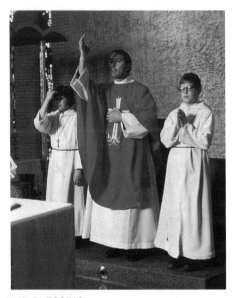

THE BLESSING

CONCLUDING RITE

WE have heard God's Word and responded to it. We have received Christ's Body and Blood and achieved greater union with Him and others. Now it is time for us to leave to praise and bless the Lord in our daily lives.

The Blessing

TO bless God means to praise Him for His goodness and wonderful gifts. To bless people is an action asking God to continue to extend His generosity over them. The priest now asks that the greatest of all benefits be given to those who have shared in God's Word and Christ's Body.

The Recessional

THE Recessional usually takes place with a song that expresses praise or reflects the particular day or season. This song is our farewell to the ministers at the altar for being helpful in reenacting and re-presenting the wondrous mystery of the Mass.

It is like the closing song of any gathering, the wish that all who came will arrive home safely, the end of a human ritual. Then we depart to try to apply the Eucharist to our lives.

THE RECESSIONAL

46

2770,
2777-
2856

The Lord's Prayer

OUR Father Who art in heaven, hallowed be Thy name; Thy kingdom come; Thy will be done on earth as it is in heaven. Give us this day our daily bread; and forgive us our trespasses as we forgive those who trespass against us; and lead us not into temptation, but deliver us from evil. Amen.

435
2676-
2678

Angelic Salutation

(Hail Mary)

HAIL, Mary, full of grace! The Lord is with you; blessed are you among women, and blessed is the fruit of your womb, Jesus. Holy Mary, Mother of God, pray for us sinners now and at the hour of our death. Amen.

2673

Morning Offering

O JESUS, through the Immaculate Heart of Mary, I offer You my prayers, works, joys and sufferings of this day for all the intentions of Your Sacred Heart, in union with the Holy Sacrifice of the Mass throughout the world, in reparation for my sins, for the intentions of all our associates, and in particular for all the intentions of this month *(mention intention if known)*.

2637

Prayer of Thanksgiving

WE give thanks to You, our Father, for the holy vine of David, Your servant, which You made known to us through Jesus Your Son. To You be glory forever.

We give thanks to You, our Father, for the life and the knowledge that You have revealed to us through Jesus Your Son. To You be glory forever.

Just as the bread that we break at Mass was once distributed on a mountain and its fragments were gathered together and became one, so too, may Your Church be gathered together from the ends of the earth into Your Kingdom. For glory and power are Yours through Jesus Christ forever.

We give thanks to You, holy Father, for Your Name, which You have made to dwell in our hearts, and for the knowledge and faith and immortality that You revealed to us through Your Son Jesus. To You be glory forever.

All-powerful Lord, You created all things for the sake of Your Name, and You gave human beings food and drink to enjoy so that they might give You thanks. Now You have favored us through Jesus Your Son with spiritual food and drink as well as with everlasting life. Above all, we give thanks to You because of Your great power. To You be glory forever.

Remember Your Church, O Lord, and deliver her from all evil. Perfect her in Your love. Then after she has been sanctified, gather her together from the four winds into the Kingdom that You have prepared for her. For the power and the glory are Yours forever.

(From the Didache)

Canticle of Mary

2639,
2673

MY soul proclaims the greatness of the Lord,
my spirit rejoices in God my Savior
for He has looked with favor on His lowly servant.
From this day all generations will call me blessed:
the Almighty has done great things for me,
and holy is His Name.
He has mercy on those who fear Him in every generation.
He has shown the strength of His arm,
He has scattered the proud in their conceit.
He has cast down the mighty from their thrones,
and has lifted up the lowly.
He has filled the hungry with good things,
and the rich He has sent away empty.

He has come to the help of His servant Israel
for He has remembered His promise of mercy,
the promise He made to our fathers,
to Abraham and his children for ever.

(Divine Office: Evening Prayer)

148, 494

The Angelus

See p. 71.

966, 971

Queen of Heaven

(Said during Eastertide instead of the Angelus)

QUEEN of heaven, rejoice, alleluia. For He Whom you merited to bear, alleluia. Has risen as He said, alleluia. Pray for us to God, alleluia.

℣. Rejoice and be glad, O Virgin Mary, alleluia.
℟. Because the Lord is truly risen, alleluia.

Let us pray. O God, Who by the Resurrection of Your Son, our Lord Jesus Christ, granted joy to the whole world, grant, we beg You, that, through the intercession of the Virgin Mary, His Mother, we may attain the joys of eternal life. Through the same Christ our Lord. Amen.

966, 971

Hail, Holy Queen

HAIL, Holy Queen, Mother of mercy, hail, our life, our sweetness, and our hope! To you do we cry, poor banished children of Eve! To you do we send up our sighs, mourning, and weeping in this vale of tears!

Turn then, most gracious advocate, your eyes of mercy toward us; and after this, our exile, show unto us the blessed fruit of your womb, Jesus! O clement, O loving, O sweet Virgin Mary!

Come, Holy Spirit, Creator Blest

2670-
2672

COME, Holy Spirit, Creator blest,
    And in our souls take up Your rest;
    Come with Your grace and heavenly aid
To fill the hearts which You have made.

O Comforter, to You we cry,
O heavenly gift of God Most High,
O fount of life and fire of love,
And sweet anointing from above.

You in Your sevenfold gifts are known;
You, finger of God's hand we own;
You, promise of the Father, You
Who do the tongue with power imbue.

Kindle our senses from above,
And make our hearts o'erflow with love;
With patience firm and virtue high
The weakness of our flesh supply.

Far from us drive the foe we dread,
And grant us Your peace instead;
So shall we not, with You for guide,
Turn from the path of life aside.

Oh, may Your grace on us bestow
The Father and the Son to know;
And You, through endless times confessed,
Of both the eternal Spirit blest.

Now to the Father and the Son,
Who rose from death, be glory given,
With You, O holy Comforter,
Henceforth by all in earth and heaven. Amen.

798,
2670-
2672
Prayer for the Seven Gifts of the Spirit

O LORD Jesus, through You I humbly beg our merciful Father to send the Holy Spirit of grace, that He may bestow upon us His sevenfold gifts.

May He send us the gift of *wisdom* which will make us relish the Tree of Life that is none other than Yourself; the gift of *understanding* which will enlighten us; the gift of *counsel* which will guide us in the way of righteousness; and the gift of *fortitude* which will give us the strength to vanquish the enemies of our sanctification and salvation.

May He impart to us the gift of *knowledge* which will enable us to discern Your teaching and distinguish good from evil; the gift of *piety* which will make us enjoy true peace; and the gift of *fear* which will make us shun all iniquity and avoid all danger of offending Your Majesty.

To the Father and to the Son and to the Holy Spirit be given all glory and thanksgiving forever.

St. Bonaventure

334-336
Prayer to One's Guardian Angel

DEAR Angel, in His goodness God gave you to me to guide, protect, and enlighten me, and to bring me back to the right way when I go astray.

Encourage me when I am disheartened, and instruct me when I err in my judgment. Help me to become more Christlike, and so some day to be accepted into the company of Angels and Saints in heaven.

436, 2683
To You, O Blessed Joseph

TO You, O blessed Joseph, do we come in our tribulation, and having implored the help of your most holy spouse, we confidently invoke your patronage also. Through that charity which bound you to the immaculate Virgin Mother of God and through the paternal love with which you embraced the Child Jesus, we humbly beg you graciously to regard the inheritance which Jesus Christ has purchased by His Blood, and with your power and strength to aid us in our necessities.

O most watchful Guardian of the Holy Family, defend the chosen children of Jesus Christ. O most loving father, ward off from us every contagion of error and corrupting influence. O our most mighty protector, be propitious to us and from heaven assist us in our struggle with the power of darkness.

And, as once you rescued the Child Jesus from deadly peril, so now protect God's Holy Church from the snares of the enemy and from all adversity. Shield, too, each one of us by your constant protection, so that, supported by your example and your aid, we may be able to live piously, to die holily, and to obtain eternal happiness in heaven. Amen.

Prayer of Ardent Longing for God   2560

O GOD, You are my God Whom I earnestly seek; for You my flesh longs and my soul thirsts as in a parched and weary land where there is no water. Hence I have gazed toward You in the sanctuary and have beheld Your power and Your glory. Because Your love is better than life, my lips will glorify You.

Thus I will bless You as long as I live; lifting up my hands, I will call upon Your Name. My soul will be satisfied as with the best of foods, and my mouth will praise You with exultant lips.

I will remember You upon my bed, and I will meditate on You through the night-watches. Because You are my help, I shout for joy in the shadow of Your wings. My soul clings close to You, and Your right hand upholds me.

Praise to God Our Father   2639

GREAT and wonderful are Your works, Lord God Almighty! Just and true are Your ways, King of the ages! Who will not fear You, O Lord, and give glory to Your Name?

For You alone are holy. All nations will come and worship before You; because Your mighty deeds are clearly seen.

2599-
2606

Jesus' Prayer for All

I DO not pray for the Apostles alone but also for those who will believe in Me through their word, that all may be one as You, Father, are in Me, and I am in You. I pray that they may be one in Us, so that the world may believe that You have sent Me.

I have given them the glory You gave Me that they may be one, even as We are one—I in them and You in Me—that their unity may be complete. So shall the world know that You sent Me and that You loved them as You loved Me.

Father, I will that where I am they also whom You have given Me may be, so that they may behold My glory, which You have given Me because of the love You bore Me before the world began.

Just Father, the world has not known You, but I have known You; and these have known that You have sent Me. I have made known to them Your Name, and I will continue to make it known so that Your love for Me may live in them, and I may live in them.

437, 2683

Prayer for the Whole Church

O GLORIOUS St. Joseph, you were chosen by God to be the foster father of Jesus, the most pure spouse of Mary, ever Virgin, and the head of the Holy Family. You have been chosen by Christ's Vicar as the heavenly Patron and Protector of the Church founded by Christ.

Protect the Sovereign Pontiff and all bishops and priests united with him. Be the protector of all who labor for souls amid the trials and tribulations of this life; and grant that all peoples of the world may follow Christ and the Church He founded.

Dear St. Joseph, accept the offering I make to you. Be my father, protector, and guide in the way of salvation. Obtain for me purity of heart and a love for the spiritual life.

After your example, let all my actions be directed to the greater glory of God, in union with the Divine Heart of Jesus, the Immaculate Heart of Mary, and your own paternal heart. Finally, pray for me that I may share in the peace and joy of your holy death.

Prayer for Priestly Vocations　　874-879

LORD our God, in Your plan for our salvation You provide shepherds for Your people. Fill Your Church with the spirit of courage and love. Raise up worthy ministers for Your altars and zealous but gentle servants of the Gospel.

Prayer for Religious Vocations　　925

LORD our God, You call all who believe in You to grow perfect in love by following in the footsteps of Christ Your Son. May those You have chosen to serve You as religious so live as to be a convincing sign of Your Kingdom for the Church and the whole world.

Prayer for the Blessing of Human Labor　　2427

ALMIGHTY God, by the labor of human beings You govern and guide to perfection the work of creation. Hear the prayers of Your people and give all persons work that enhances their human dignity while drawing them closer to each other in the service of their brothers and sisters.

Prayer for the Nation, State, or City　　2234

LORD our God, You guide everything in wisdom and love. Accept the prayers we offer for our nation (or state, or city). By the wisdom of our leaders and integrity of our citizens, may harmony and justice be secured and lasting prosperity and peace be attained.

2235

Prayer for Those Who Serve in Public Office

ALMIGHTY and eternal God, You know the longings of human hearts and You protect their rights. In Your goodness, watch over those in authority, so that people everywhere may enjoy freedom, security, and peace.

1508,
1519

Prayer for the Sick

HEAVENLY Father, Your Son accepted our sufferings to teach us the virtue of patience in human illness. Hear the prayers we offer for our sick brothers and sisters. May all who suffer pain, illness, or disease realize that they are chosen to be Saints and that they are joined to Christ in His suffering for the salvation of the world.

2299

Prayer for the Dying

GOD of power and mercy, You have made death itself the gateway to eternal life. Look with love on our dying brother / sister, and make him / her one with Your Son in His suffering and death. Then, sealed with the blood of Christ, may he / she come before You free from sin.

1524

Prayer for a Holy Death

O CHRIST, let me confess Your Name with my last breath. In Your great mercy receive me and do not disappoint me in my hope. Open the gates of life for me, and let the prince of darkness have no power over me.

Protect me by Your kindness, shield me with Your might, and lead me by Your right hand to the place of refreshment, the tabernacle You have prepared for Your servants and for those who revere You.

Prayer to Do Always the Will of God

2098,
2611

O LORD, regulate all things by Your wisdom, so that I may always serve You in the manner that You will rather than in the manner that I will. Do not punish me by granting what I will if it offends against Your love, for I want Your love to live always in me. Help me to deny myself in order that I may serve You. Let me live for You—Who in Yourself are the true Life.

Prayer for the Strength to Repent

976,
2608,

FATHER in heaven, the light of Jesus has scattered the darkness of hatred and sin. Called to that light we ask for Your guidance. Form our lives in Your truth, our hearts in Your love.

Prayer of Sorrow for Sin

981

LORD Jesus hanging on the Cross, I raise sorrowful and shameful eyes to You. You have granted me untold blessings and I have repaid You by contributing to Your Passion and death. My hands took part in Your scourging, my voice was among those who denied You and called for Your death, my thoughts brought about Your crowning with thorns, my sins drove the nails into Your hands and feet, and the lance into Your side.

Dear Lord, forgive me for all these sins. You are great, glorious, and infinitely good; I am insignificant, selfish, and hopelessly sinful. But I am sorry for all my sins, and by the Blood shed in Your Passion I beg for forgiveness and for a share in Your love and grace.

Prayer for Pardon and Peace

987

OUT of the depths I cry to You, O Lord; Lord, hear my voice! Let Your ears be attentive to my cry for mercy. If You, O Lord, mark iniquities, Lord, who can stand? But with You there is forgiveness; therefore You are revered.

I trust in the Lord; my soul trusts in His word. My soul waits for the Lord more than watchmen wait for the dawn.

More than watchmen wait for the dawn, let Israel wait for the Lord. For with the Lord is unfailing love and with Him is full redemption. He will redeem Israel from all their iniquities.

2631,
2838

Prayer for Forgiveness

O GOD, mercy and forgiveness are Yours by nature and by right. Receive our humble petitions. Though we are bound tightly by the chain of our sins, set us free by the power of Your great mercy.

302-305

Prayer for God's Continued Providence

A LMIGHTY Lord, the hand of Your loving kindness powerfully yet gently guides all the moments of our day. Go before us in our pilgrimage of life, anticipate our needs, and prevent our falling. Send Your Spirit to unite us in faith, that, sharing in Your service, we may rejoice in Your presence.

2633

Prayer for Rain

L ORD God, in You we live and move and have our being. Help us in our present time of trouble, send us the rain we need, and teach us to seek Your lasting help on the way to eternal life.

310, 2633

Prayer in Time of Earthquake

L ORD God, You set the earth on its foundation. Keep us safe from the danger of earthquakes and let us always feel the presence of Your love. May we be secure in Your protection and serve You with grateful hearts.

Prayer to Overcome Prejudice   2317

A LMIGHTY God, Your care extends beyond the boundaries of race and nation to the hearts of all who live. May the walls that prejudice raises between us crumble beneath the power of Your outstretched arm.

Prayer to Bring Christ's Peace to the World   2305

A LMIGHTY God, Your Word, Jesus Christ, spoke peace to a sinful world and brought humankind the gift of reconciliation by the suffering and death He endured. Teach us who bear His name to follow the example He gave us. May our faith, hope, and love turn hatred to love, conflict to peace, and death to eternal life.

Prayer of Extraordinary Ministers of Communion   1348

H EAVENLY Father, I thank You for calling me to serve You and Your people in this community as an extraordinary minister of the Eucharist. You know that I could never be worthy of such an exalted honor. Help me to be less unworthy by remaining free from sin.

Let me nourish Your people with the witness of my life as I feed them with the Body of Christ. Grant Your strength and holiness to all Your extraordinary ministers and make them worthy to bring Christ to others.

Prayer to the Infant Jesus   525-530

O LORD Christ, You were pleased so to humble Yourself in Your incarnate Divinity and most sacred Humanity, as to be born in time and become a little child. Grant that we may acknowledge infinite wisdom in the silence of a child, power in weakness, and majesty in humiliation. Adoring Your humiliations on earth, may we contemplate Your glories in heaven.

968-969

Prayer to Our Lady of Perpetual Help

O MOTHER of Perpetual Help, grant that I may ever invoke your powerful name, which is the safeguard of the living and the salvation of the dying. O pure Virgin Mary, let your name be henceforth ever on my lips. Whenever I call on you by name, hasten to help me. When I speak your sacred name or even think of you, what consolation and confidence, what sweetness and emotion fill my soul!

I thank God for having given you so sweet, powerful, and lovely a name for my good. Let my love for you prompt me ever to greet you as Mother of Perpetual Help.

1816,
2683

Prayer to St. Jude

Patron of Desperate Cases

O GLORIOUS St. Jude, you were honored to be a cousin as well as a follower of Jesus, and you wrote an Epistle in which you said: "Grow strong in your holy faith through prayer in the Holy Spirit." Obtain for us the grace of being people of faith and people of prayer. Let us be so attached to the three Divine Persons through faith and prayer on earth that we may be united with them in the glory of the Beatific Vision in heaven.

2002,
2683

Prayer to St. Anthony of Padua

Patron of All Who Seek Lost Articles

D EAR St. Anthony, you are the patron of the poor and the helper of all who seek lost articles. Help me to find the object I have lost so that I will be able to make better use of the time that I will gain for God's greater honor and glory. Grant your gracious aid to all people who seek what they have lost—especially those who seek to regain God's grace.

Prayer to St. Gerard Majella
Patron of Expectant Mothers

1653,
2683

DEAR Redemptorist Saint, model Priest and Religious, compassionate toward suffering Mothers intercede for this expectant Mother. Let her not be selfish like those who are willing to put an end to the life they bear within themselves. Instead let her remain ever conscious that she is privileged to be the instrument through whom God brings another life into the world. Encourage her for the good of her child and the glory of the Lord of life.

Prayer to St. Peregrine
Patron of Cancer Patients

1472,
2683

DEAR Apostle of Emilia and member of the Order of Mary, you spread the Good News by your word and by your life witnessed to its truth. In union with Jesus crucified, you endured excruciating sufferings so patiently as to be healed miraculously of cancer in the leg. If it is agreeable to God, obtain relief and cure for N.... and keep us all from the dread cancer of sin.

Prayer to St. Charles Borromeo
Patron of Catechists

906,
2683

O SAINTLY reformer, animator of spiritual renewal of priests and religious, you organized true seminaries and wrote a standard catechism. Inspire all religious teachers and authors of catechetical books. Move them to love and transmit only that which can form true followers of the Teacher Who was divine.

Prayer to St. Aloysius
Patron of Youth

2211,
2683

DEAR Christian youth, you were a faithful follower of Christ in the Society of Jesus. You steadily strove for perfection while generously serving the plague-stricken. Help our youth today who are faced with a plague of false cults and false gods. Show them how to harness their energies and to use them for their own and others' fulfillment—which will redound to the greater glory of God.

158, 2683

Prayer to St. Thomas Aquinas
Patron of Students

WONDERFUL theologian and Doctor of the Church, you learned more from the Crucifix than from books. Combining both sources, you left us the marvelous *Summa* of theology, broadcasting most glorious enlightenment to all. You always sought for true light and studied for God's honor and glory. Help us all to study our religion as well as all other subjects needed for life, without ambition and pride in imitation of you.

849, 2683

Prayer to St. John Baptist de la Salle
Patron of Educators

WELL-KNOWN Founder of the Congregation of the Brothers of Christian Schools, orthodox and prayerful theologian, you realized the very great value of competent Christian educators. How great your wholesome influence has been! Make your followers continue to be Christ-like models for all their students who in turn will edify others.

2427-
2428,
2683

Prayer to St. Joseph
Patron of Workers

DEAR Patron of God's Church, you are honored by her as the Worker, the humble carpenter of Nazareth. According to St. Teresa of Avila, you are universal in your intercessions. Inspire workers of all kinds to walk ever in your footsteps as faithful servants coupling charity with justice and becoming true followers of Jesus.

Prayer to St. Isidore the Farmer
Patron of Farmers

2427,
2683

DEAR Isidore, you know how normal it is to cultivate the land for you were employed as a farm laborer for the greater part of your life. Although you received God's help materially through Angels in the field, all farmers are aided spiritually to see the wonders God has strewn on this earth. Encourage all farmers in their labors and help them to feed numerous people.

Prayer before Reading the Bible

133

COME, Holy Spirit, fill the hearts of your faithful and enkindle in them the fire of Your love.

℣. Send forth Your Spirit and they shall be created.
℟. And You shall renew the face of the earth.

Let us pray. O God, You instructed the hearts of the faithful by the light of the Holy Spirit. Grant us by the same Spirit to have a right judgment in all things and ever to rejoice in His consolation. Through Christ our Lord.

Prayer after Reading the Bible

133

LET me not, O Lord, be puffed up with worldly wisdom, which passes away. Grant me that love which never abates, that I may not choose to know anything among men but Jesus, and Him crucified.

I pray You, loving Jesus, that as You have graciously given me to drink in with delight the words of Your knowledge, so You would mercifully grant me to attain one day to You, the Fountain of all wisdom, and to appear forever before Your face.

1691,
1716

Introduction

AS community of faith members, individual Catholics live out their beliefs according to God's word, especially as it is manifest in the commandments of God. We believe that if we dismiss the word of God's command we will not receive the word of His grace. In order to better assist its members in living God's commandments, the Church has developed a number of precepts. Moreover, we learn of the spiritual and corporal works of mercy that facilitate the unity of our faith community.

Naturally, there are individual differences and needs that have been recognized in a variety of practices, devotions, and activities that address the spiritual inclinations of the multifaceted faith community. For example, the Rosary is a widely used form of prayer and devotion to the Blessed Mother. Also, First Friday devotions over the past few centuries have played a substantial devotional role in the life of the Church.

Thus, we see presented here a grouping of widely accepted practices both required and voluntary. Finally, an overview of the Books of Scripture and the history of the Catholic Church in the United States are provided.

2052,
2075

The Ten Commandments

1. I, the Lord, am your God. You shall not have other gods besides Me.
2. You shall not take the name of the Lord, your God, in vain.
3. Remember to keep holy the Sabbath day.
4. Honor your father and your mother.
5. You shall not kill.
6. You shall not commit adultery.
7. You shall not steal.

8. You shall not bear false witness against your neighbor.
9. You shall not covet your neighbor's wife.
10. You shall not covet your neighbor's goods.

Precepts of the Church
(Traditional Form)

2041-43

1. To participate at Mass on all Sundays and Holydays of Obligation.
2. To fast and to abstain on the days appointed.
3. To confess our sins at least once a year.
4. To receive Holy Communion during the Easter time.
5. To contribute to the support of the Church.
6. To observe the laws of the Church concerning marriage.

(Long Form)

2041-2043

From time to time the Church has listed certain specific duties of Catholics. Among those expected of Catholic Christians today are the following. (Those traditionally mentioned as Precepts of the Church are marked with an asterisk.)

1. To keep holy the day of the Lord's Resurrection: to worship God by participating in Mass every Sunday and Holy Day of Obligation;* to avoid those activities that would hinder renewal of soul and body on the Sabbath (e.g., needless work and business activities, unnecessary shopping, etc.).

2. To lead a Sacramental life: to receive Holy Communion frequently and the Sacrament of Reconciliation regularly— minimally, to receive the Sacrament of Reconciliation at least once a year (annual confession is obligatory only if serious sin is involved);*—minimally also, to receive Holy Communion at least once a year, between the First Sunday of Lent and Trinity Sunday.*

3. To study Catholic teaching in preparation for the Sacrament of Confirmation, to be confirmed, and then to continue to study and advance the cause of Christ.

4. To observe the marriage laws of the Church;* to give religious training, by example and word, to one's children; to use parish schools and catechetical programs.

5. To strengthen and support the Church*—one's own parish community and parish priests, the worldwide Church and the Pope.

6. To do penance, including abstaining from meat and fasting from food on the appointed days.*

7. To join in the missionary spirit and apostolate of the Church.

Days of Fast and Abstinence

1434,
2043

O N the days of fast we must limit ourselves to one full meal. In addition to one full meal, two lighter meals are allowed. But snacking between meals breaks the fast and the precept.

The law of fast is binding on Catholics from age 21 to 59 inclusive. The sick (including pregnant women) are not bound by the precept. Other persons also may have sufficient grounds for being excused; e.g., if by fasting they cannot meet the demands of their regular work. In doubt, we may consult a priest, confessor, or any competent and trustworthy person.

In the United States, the days of fast prescribed by the Church are: Ash Wednesday and Good Friday.

On days of abstinence we must abstain from meat. The law of abstinence is binding on Catholics from age 14; there is no upper limit. Conditions of health, unavailability of meatless fare, etc., may excuse a person.

In the United States, Friday remains a day of penance and the tradition of abstinence from meat has primary place although an alternate penance or work of charity may be chosen.

By obligation, Ash Wednesday, Good Friday and all other Fridays of Lent are days of abstinence from meat.

While modifying the penitential practices of the past remembered by many older Catholics, the Church continues to teach the necessity of penance in the life of every Christian.

Spiritual Works of Mercy

2447-
2448

1. To admonish the sinner (correct those who need it).
2. To instruct the ignorant (teach the ignorant).
3. To counsel the doubtful (give advice to those who need it).
4. To comfort the sorrowful (comfort those who suffer).
5. To bear wrongs patiently (be patient with others).
6. To forgive all injuries (forgive others who hurt you).
7. To pray for the living and the dead (pray for others).

Corporal Works of Mercy

2447-
2449

1. To feed the hungry.
2. To give drink to the thirsty.
3. To clothe the naked.
4. To visit the imprisoned.
5. To shelter the homeless.
6. To visit the sick.
7. To bury the dead.

Holy Days of Obligation

2042

Holy Days in the United States

New Year's Day (Mary, Mother of God) .January 1
Ascension Thursday ....40 days after Easter
Assumption of Mary into heaven.............August 15
All Saints Day...November 1
Immaculate Conception of Mary.............December 8
Christmas ....December 25

Holy Days in the Church

2042,
2177

HOLY Days of Obligation are special feasts for Catholics. Formerly there were many more, but the industrial age led to a curtailment of the number. At the present time, there are ten Holy Days of Obligation listed for the Universal Church, but each Episcopal Conference is free to reduce these in view of the circumstances of its particular country and people. The ten include the six days listed above plus: Epiphany (January 6), Corpus Christi (Thursday after Trinity Sunday), Solemnity of St. Joseph (March 19), and Solemnity of Sts. Peter and Paul (June 29).

The Church in America celebrates two of the additional four Holy Days on Sundays (Epiphany and Corpus Christi). Thus, there are only two of the ten that are not Holy Days of Obligation in the United States (St. Joseph and Sts. Peter and Paul). However, the American Bishops recently gave some thought to a proposal to reduce the Holy Days for the reason, among others, that too many people must work and cannot observe them properly. Nevertheless, popular reaction was negative and the proposal was shelved.

The Liturgical Year

1168-1171

THE Liturgical Year is the succession of Seasons and Feasts of the Church celebrated annually from Advent to Advent.

As presently constituted, the Liturgical Year has the following Seasons (divisions):

Advent: This Season begins about four weeks before Christmas. It comprises four Sundays. The Sunday that falls on November 30, or is closest to it, is the First Sunday of Advent.

Christmas Time: This Season runs from the Solemnity of Christmas until the Sunday after Epiphany or after January 6, inclusive. The period from the end of Christmas Time until the beginning of Lent is included in the Ordinary Time of the year (see below).

Lent: The Penitential Season of Lent begins on Ash Wednesday and continues until Easter. The final week is called Holy Week, and its last three days are called the Paschal (Easter) Triduum.

Easter Time: This Season spans a 50-day period, from the Solemnity of Easter to Pentecost. Its central theme is the Resurrection of Christ together with our resurrection from sin to the new life of grace.

Ordinary Time: This Season comprises the other 33 or 34

weeks of the Liturgical Year. It includes not only the period between the end of Christmas Time and the beginning of Lent but all Sundays and weekdays after Pentecost until the beginning of Advent. It is "ordinary" only by comparison, because the great Feasts of our Lord are prepared for and specially celebrated other times of the year.

Feasts: The first Christians knew only one Feast, Easter, the Feast of our Lord's Resurrection. But this they celebrated all the time, whenever they gathered for the Eucharist. In the Eucharistic celebration, every day and especially every Sunday became for them a little Easter. Easter, in fact, is the center in which all Mysteries of our Redemption merge.

Eventually, however, the Church began to celebrate many of these mysteries in their own right, with feasts of their own, especially the Birth of our Lord, His Life and Death as well as His Resurrection and Glorification, and also the sending of the Holy Spirit and His work of grace in the soul. Gradually added were Feasts of the Blessed Mother Mary and the Saints.

The Liturgical Year, therefore, has had a long history of development. As early as the year 700, however, the Roman Liturgical Year was essentially as it is today, with two major cycles, Christmas with its Advent and Easter with its Lent, plus the Sundays in between.

Participation in the Liturgy

(See also pp. 39-46)

1140-
1144

In liturgical celebrations (such as the Mass, the Sacraments, and the Sacramentals), *each person has an office to perform.* The *people* take part by means of acclamations, responses, psalmody, antiphons, and songs, as well as by actions, gestures, bodily attitudes, and a reverent silence at the proper times.

The distribution of liturgical roles is of the highest importance as a sign. It shows that the Assembly is a manifestation of the Church, one of whose essential qualities is a *hierarchi-*

cal structure of persons differing in rank and function.

All Catholics are called to celebrate the Liturgy by a *full, conscious, and active participation* that is both external and internal as well as Sacramental (through Communion).

Regulations for Holy Communion

1355,
1385-
1388

THE conditions for receiving Holy Communion are: (1) the state of grace, (2) the right intention, (3) and the Eucharistic fast.

State of grace: freedom from mortal sin. But our Communions will bring more grace and blessing, and our spiritual growth in Christ will be greater, if we also strive to overcome venial sin in our life.

Right intention: not out of habit or human respect, but to please God and to live a better Catholic life.

Eucharistic fast: abstaining from food and drink (water excepted) one hour before Holy Communion. Plain water never breaks the fast. In addition, the sick and aged need fast only 15 minutes. The sick, moreover, if their condition requires, may take non-alcoholic beverages and solid or liquid medicine before Holy Communion without any time limit.

Nowadays, happily, faithful Catholics are receiving Holy Communion more than in the past, regularly on Sundays for many and also daily in goodly number. For such persons the Communion precept offers no problem. They will be receiving Holy Communion as a matter of course during Easter Time. Nor is it necessary for them to designate a particular Communion of that period as their Easter Communion.

Going to Confession

1422,
1455-
1460

THE Sacrament of Penance has a rite, that is, a format in which the Sacrament is celebrated by use of various signs or symbols, gestures, words, and the like. It consists of the following: (1) reception of the penitent, (2) reading of the Word of God, (3) confession of sins and acceptance of satisfaction, (4) prayer of the penitent and absolution, and (5) proclamation of praise of God and dismissal.

Before celebrating the Sacrament, both confessors and penitents should prepare themselves above all by prayer. Priests should have recourse to the Holy Spirit for light and charity. Penitents should examine their lives in the light of Christ's example and commandments and then pray to God for forgiveness.

(1) Welcoming the Penitents. Priests should welcome penitents with love and speak to them in friendship. Then the penitents make the Sign of the Cross and the priests—by a short formula—urge them to have confidence in God. Penitents who are not known to the confessors should indicate their state in life, the time of their last Confession, their difficulties in leading a Christian life, and any other particulars that may help the confessors to carry out their ministry.

(2) Reading of the Word of God. Next the priests or penitents may read a text from Sacred Scripture (if it has not already been done as a preparation for the Sacrament). Through the Word of God Christians are illumined to recognize their sins and summoned to conversion and confidence in God's mercy.

(3) Confession of Sins and Acceptance of Satisfaction. The penitents now confess their sins. If need be, the confessors help them make an integral confession and to have sincere sorrow for their sins. Finally, they offer the penitents suitable advice for beginning a new life and may even instruct them in the duties of the Christian life.

If the penitents have harmed or scandalized others, the confessors should exact from them a resolve to make restitution.

Then the confessors impose an act of penance or satisfaction which serves not only to expiate the penitents' sins but also aids them to begin a new life. The penance should correspond as far as possible to the gravity and nature of the sins committed. It may be a prayer, an act of self-denial, some service rendered to a neighbor, or a work of mercy—stressing the social aspect of sin and forgiveness.

(4) The Prayer of the Penitents and Absolution. A prayer for

God's forgiveness manifests the penitents' contrition and resolve to begin a new life. Then the priests extend their hands
(or at least one hand) on the head of the penitents and pro-
nounce the formula of absolution.

"God, the Father of mercies, through the death and resurrection of His Son has reconciled the world to Himself and
sent the Holy Spirit among us for the forgiveness of sins;
through the ministry of the Church may God give you pardon
and peace, and I absolve you from your sins in the name of the
Father, and of the Son, ✚ and of the Holy Spirit."

The essential words are: "I absolve you from your sins in
the name of the Father, and of the Son, and of the Holy Spirit."

(5) Proclamation of Praise and Dismissal. After receiving
forgiveness, the penitents praise God's mercy and give Him
thanks by means of a short text taken from Sacred Scripture.
Then the confessors tell them to go in peace.

Penitents continue their conversion and express it by a life
renewed in accord with the Gospel and steeped in God's love,
for "love covers a multitude of sins" (1 Pt 4:8).

In accord with pastoral needs, some parts of this rite may
be shortened or even omitted. However, confession of sins and
the acceptance of the act of penance as well as the invitation
to contrition and the form of absolution and dismissal must be
retained in their entirety. When there is imminent danger of
death, the essential words of the form of absolution suffice: "I
absolve you from your sins in the name of the Father, and of
the Son, and of the Holy Spirit."

The Angelus

971

IT is a holy tradition to pray at morning, noon, and night.
The Angelus is part of this tradition and seems to have
been inspired, indirectly, by the Liturgy of the Hours. The
church bells were rung when the monks prayed the hours of
Lauds (Morning Prayer) and Vespers (Evening Prayer). At
each ringing the people of the countryside, wanting to join in
the prayer of the monks, prayed something at home. The be-

ginnings of this custom can be traced to the early 14th century, but the present form of the Angelus dates to the 17th. During the Easter season, instead of the Angelus the Regina Caeli or Queen of Heaven is said (see p. 49).

℣. The Angel of the Lord declared unto Mary.

℟. And she conceived of the Holy Spirit.
   Hail Mary, etc.

℣. Behold the handmaid of the Lord.

℟. Be it done to me according to your word.
   Hail Mary, etc.

℣. And the Word was made flesh.

℟. And dwelt among us.
   Hail Mary, etc.

℣. Pray for us, O holy Mother of God.

℟. That we may be made worthy of the promises of Christ.

Let us pray. Pour forth, we beg You, O Lord, Your grace into our hearts: that we, to whom the Incarnation of Christ Your Son was made known by the message of an Angel, may by His Passion and Cross be brought to the glory of His Resurrection. Through the same Christ our Lord. ℟. Amen.

Grace before Meals

B LESS us, O Lord, and these Your gifts which we are about to receive from Your bounty. Through Christ our Lord. Amen.
2626, 2698

Grace after Meals

W E give You thanks, Almighty God, for all Your benefits, and may the souls of the faithful departed, through the mercy of God, rest in peace. Amen.
2637, 2698

435, 971, 2676- 2678, 2708

The Holy Rosary

THE devotion of the Holy Rosary has been treasured in the Church for centuries. It is a summary of Christian faith in language and prayers inspired by the Bible. It calls to mind the most important events in the lives of Jesus and Mary. These events are called Mysteries and are divided into three groups of decades. They are: the five Joyful, the five Sorrowful, and the five Glorious Mysteries. Each decade consists of one "Our Father," ten "Hail Marys," and one "Glory be to the Father."

HOW TO SAY THE ROSARY

1. Begin on the crucifix and say the Apostles' Creed.
2. On the 1st bead, say 1 Our Father.
3. On the next 3 beads, say Hail Mary.
4. Next say 1 Glory Be. Then announce and think of the first Mystery and say 1 Our Father.
5. Say 10 Hail Marys and 1 Glory be to the Father.
6. Announce the second Mystery and continue in the same way until each of the five Mysteries of the selected group or decades is said.

971

Prayer before the Rosary

O MOST holy Virgin Mary, Queen of the most holy Rosary, you were pleased to appear to the children of Fatima and reveal a glorious message. We implore you, inspire in our hearts a fervent love for the recitation of the Rosary. By meditating on the mysteries of the redemption that are recalled therein may we obtain the graces and virtues that we ask, through the merits of Jesus Christ, our Lord and Redeemer.

The Five Joyful Mysteries

(Said on Mondays, T̶h̶u̶r̶s̶d̶a̶y̶s̶, the Sundays of Advent, and Sundays from Epiphany until Lent)

The Joyful Mysteries direct our mind to the Son of God, Jesus Christ, our Lord and Savior, Who took human nature from a human mother, Mary. They also bring to our attention some of the extraordinary events that preceded, accompanied, and followed Christ's birth.

1. The Annunciation
Lk 1:26-38; Is 7:10-15

488, 494

MARY, you received with deep humility the news of the Angel Gabriel that you were to be the Mother of God's Son; obtain for me a similar *humility.*

2. The Visitation
Lk 1:41-50

523

MARY, you showed true charity in visiting Elizabeth and remaining with her for three months before the birth of John the Baptist; obtain for me the grace to *love my neighbor.*

3. The Birth of Jesus
Lk 2:1-14; Mt 2:1-14; Gal 4:1-7

525

JESUS, You lovingly accepted poverty when You were placed in the manger in the stable although You were our God and Redeemer; grant that I may have the *spirit of poverty.*

4. The Presentation in the Temple
Lk 2:22-40

529

MARY, you obeyed the law of God in presenting the Child Jesus in the Temple; obtain for me the *virtue of obedience.*

534

5. The Finding in the Temple
Lk 2:42-52

MARY, you were filled with sorrow at the loss of Jesus and overwhelmed with joy on finding Him surrounded by Teachers in the Temple; obtain for me the *virtue of piety*.

The Five Sorrowful Mysteries

(Said on Tuesdays and Fridays throughout the year, and daily from Ash Wednesday until Easter Sunday)

The Sorrowful Mysteries recall to our mind the mysterious events surrounding Christ's sacrifice of His life in order that sinful humanity might be reconciled with God.

612

1. The Agony in the Garden
Mt 26:36-40

JESUS, in the Garden of Gethsemani, You suffered a bitter agony because of our sins; grant me *true contrition*.

572

2. The Scourging at the Pillar
Mt 27:24-26; 1 Pt 2:21-25

JESUS, You endured a cruel scourging and Your flesh was torn by heavy blows; help me to have the *virtue of purity*.

595

3. The Crowning with Thorns
Mt 26:27-31

JESUS, You patiently endured the pain from the crown of sharp thorns that was forced upon Your head; grant me the strength to have *moral courage*.

596

4. The Carrying of the Cross
Mt 27:32

JESUS, You willingly carried Your Cross for love of Your Father and all people; grant me the *virtue of patience*.

5. The Crucifixion
Mt 27:33-50; Jn 19:31-37

616

JESUS, for love of me You endured three hours of torture on the Cross and gave up Your spirit; grant me the grace of *final perseverance.*

The Five Glorious Mysteries

(Said on Wednesdays and Saturdays, and the Sundays from Easter until Advent)

The Glorious Mysteries recall to our mind the ratification of Christ's sacrifice for the redemption of the world, and our sharing in the fruits of His sacrifice.

1. The Resurrection
Mk 16:1-7; Jn 20:19-31

638

JESUS, You rose from the dead in triumph and remained for forty days with Your disciples, instructing and encouraging them; increase my *faith.*

2. The Ascension
Mk 16:14-20; Acts 1:1-11

659

JESUS, in the presence of Mary and the disciples You ascended to heaven to sit at the Father's right hand; increase the *virtue of hope* in me.

3. The Descent of the Holy Spirit
Jn 14:23-31; Acts 2:1-11

731

JESUS, in fulfillment of Your promise You sent the Holy Spirit upon Mary and the disciple's under the form of tongues of fire; increase my *love for God.*

4. The Assumption
Lk 1:41-50; Ps 45; Gn 3:15

966

MARY, by the power of God you were assumed into heaven and united with your Divine Son; help me to have *true devotion to you.*

969

5. The Crowning of the Blessed Virgin
Rv 12:1; Jdt 13:22-25

MARY, you were crowned Queen of heaven by Your Divine Son to the great joy of all the Saints; obtain *eternal happiness* for me.

At the end of the Rosary, one may add the prayer "Hail, Holy Queen," p. 49, and the following prayer:

971

Prayer after the Rosary

O GOD, Whose only-begotten Son, by His Life, Death, and Resurrection, has purchased for us the rewards of eternal life; grant, we beseech You, that, meditating upon these mysteries of the Most Holy Rosary of the Blessed Virgin Mary, we may imitate what they contain and obtain what they promise, through the same Christ our Lord.

74, 410,
2782

Rosary of the Divine Mercy

The Rosary of the Divine Mercy is recited on an ordinary rosary. We can say it preferably for the great intentions of the Church and the world: the unity of Christians, the conversion of sinners, the return of a nation to God, peace among human beings, and the like.

On the single bead, say:

HOLY Father, I offer You the Body and Blood, Soul and Divinity of Your Son Jesus in reparation for our sins and the sins of the whole world.

On each of the ten beads (decade), say:

BY His sorrowful Passion, have pity on us and on the whole world.

At the end of each decade, say:

HOLY God, mighty God, eternal God, have mercy on us.

At the end of the Rosary, say:

BLOOD and water that issued from the Heart of Jesus as the Source of mercy for us, I put my trust in You.

First Friday Devotions in Honor of the Sacred Heart

477-478

FAITHFUL Catholics consecrate to the Sacred Heart of Jesus, in the spirit of reparation, the First Friday of each month. Jesus Himself made the following promises to St. Margaret Mary in favor of those who practice and promote this devotion.

1. I will give them all the graces necessary in their state of life.

2. I will establish peace in their homes.

3. I will comfort them in all their afflictions.

4. I will be their secure refuge during life, and above all in death.

5. I will bestow abundant blessings upon all their undertakings.

6. Sinners shall find in My Heart the source and the infinite ocean of mercy.

7. Tepid souls shall become fervent.

8. Fervent souls shall quickly mount to high perfection.

9. I will bless every place in which an image of My Heart shall be exposed and honored.

10. I will give the priests the gift of touching the most hardened hearts.

11. Those who shall promote this devotion shall have their names written in My Heart, never to be effaced.

12. I promise you in the excessive mercy of My Heart that My all-powerful love will grant to all those who communicate on the First Friday in nine consecutive months the grace of

final penitence; they shall not die in My disgrace nor without receiving their Sacraments. My divine Heart shall be their safe refuge in this last moment.

956, 2683

Novena of Grace in Honor of St. Francis Xavier

O VERY dear St. Francis Xavier, full of divine charity, with you I reverently adore the divine Majesty. Since I greatly rejoice in the singular gifts of grace that the Lord conferred on you in this life, and of glory after death, I return most heartfelt thanks to Him, and I beg of you to obtain for me, by your powerful intercession, above all the grace to live well and die holily.

Moreover, I ask you to gain for me *(here insert your petition).* But if that which I suppliantly ask of you is not for the greater glory of God and the greater good of my soul, I beg you to obtain for me whatever will better promote both these ends.

Our Father, Hail Mary, Glory be, etc.

599-618,
1674

Scriptural Way of the Cross

The Way of the Cross is a devotion in which we meditate on Christ's Passion and Death in order to put their meaning into our lives. This Passion and Death are "revelations" of the love of God the Father for all people and of Christ's love for the Father and all people. The devotion of the Way of the Cross should lead us to do in our lives what Jesus did—we must give our lives in the service of others.

601, 618

Opening Prayer

H EAVENLY Father, grant that we who meditate on the Passion and Death of Your Son, Jesus Christ, may imitate in our lives His love and self-giving to You and to others. We ask this through Christ our Lord.

1. Jesus is Condemned to Death   595
Jn 3:16f; Is 53:7; Jn 15:13

GOD so loved the world that He gave His only Son, . . . that the world might be saved through Him.

Although He was harshly treated, He submitted and opened not His mouth. He was silent and opened not his mouth, like a lamb led to the slaughter or a sheep before the shearers.

There is no greater love than this: to lay down one's life for one's friends.

Let us pray.

Father, in the flesh of Your Son You condemned sin. Grant us the gift of eternal life in the same Christ our Lord.

2. Jesus Bears His Cross   616
Is 53:4; Lk 9:23; Mt 11:28f

IT was our infirmities that He bore, our sufferings that He endured.

Those who wish to be My followers must deny their very selves, take up the their cross each day, and follow in My steps.

Take My yoke upon your shoulders and learn from Me, . . . for My yoke is easy and My burden light.

Let us pray.

Father, Your Son Jesus humbled Himself and became obedient to death. Teach us to glory above all else in the Cross, in which is our salvation. Grant this through Christ our Lord.

3. Jesus Falls the First Time   623
Lam 3:16f; Is 53:6; Jn 1:29

HE has broken My teeth with gravel, pressed My face in the dust; My soul is deprived of peace, I have forgotten what happiness is.

The Lord laid upon Him the guilt of us all. Behold the Lamb of God Who takes away the sin of the world.

Let us pray.

Father, help us to remain unreprehensible in Your sight, so that we can offer You our body as a holy and living offering. We ask this in the name of Jesus the Lord.

964

4. Jesus Meets His Mother
Lk 2:49; Lam 1:12; Jn 16:22

D ID you not know I had to be in My Father's house? Come, all you who pass by the way, look and see whether there is any suffering like My suffering.

You are sad for a time, but I shall see you again. Then your hearts will rejoice with a joy no one can take from you.

Let us pray.

Father, accept the sorrows of the Blessed Virgin Mary, Mother of Your Son. May they obtain from Your mercy every good for our salvation.

572

5. Jesus Is Helped by Simon
Mt 25:40; Gal 6:2; Jn 13:16

A S often as you did it for one of My least brothers and sisters, you did it for Me.

Help carry one another's burdens; in that way you will fulfill the law of Christ. No servant is greater than his master.

Let us pray.

Father, You have first loved us and You sent Your Son to expiate our sins. Grant that we may love one another and bear each other's burdens. We ask this through Christ our Lord.

573

6. Veronica Wipes the Face of Jesus
Is 52:14; Jn 14:9; Heb 1:3

H IS look was marred beyond that of man, and His appearance beyond that of mortals.
Whoever has seen Me has seen the Father.

The Son is the reflection of the Father's glory, the exact representation of the Father's being.

Let us pray.

Heavenly Father, grant that we may reflect Your Son's glory and be transformed into His image so that we may be configured to Him. We ask this in the name of Jesus.

7. Jesus Falls a Second Time   598
Ps 118:3; Heb 4:15; Mt 11:28

I WAS hard pressed and was falling, but the Lord helped Me.

We do not have a priest Who is unable to sympathize with our weakness, but one Who was tempted in every way that we are, yet never sinned.

Come to Me, all you who are weary and find life burdensome, and I will refresh you.

Let us pray.

God our Father, grant that we may walk in the footsteps of Jesus Who suffered for us and redeemed us not with gold and silver but with the price of His own blood. We ask this through Christ our Lord.

8. Jesus Speaks to the Women   601
Lk 23:28; Jn 15:6; Lk 13:3

DAUGHTERS of Jerusalem, do not weep for Me. Weep for yourselves and for your children.

Whoever does not live in Me is like a withered, rejected branch.

You will all come to the same end as some Galileans who perished unless you reform.

Let us pray.

Heavenly Father, You desire to show mercy rather than anger toward all who hope in You. Grant that we may weep for our sins and merit the grace of Your glory. We ask this in the name of Jesus the Lord.

602

9. Jesus Falls a Third Time
Ps 22:15f; Phil 2:5-7; Lk 14:11

I AM like water poured out; all My bones are out of joint. My heart has become like wax. My throat is dried up like baked clay, My tongue sticks to the roof of My mouth. You have brought Me down to the dust of death.

Your attitude must be that of Christ: . . . He emptied Himself and took the form of a servant.

All who exalt themselves shall be humbled and those who humble themselves shall be exalted.

Let us pray.

God our Father, look with pity on us oppressed by the weight of our sins and grant us Your forgiveness. Help us to serve You with our whole heart. We ask this through Christ our Lord.

603

10. Jesus Is Stripped of His Garments
Ps 22:19; Lk 14:33; Rom 13:14

THEY divide My garments among them, and for My vesture they cast lots.

None of you can be My disciple if you do not renounce all your possessions.

Put on the Lord Jesus Christ and do not think about how to gratify the desires of the flesh.

Let us pray.

Heavenly Father, let nothing deprive us of Your love—neither trials nor distress nor persecution. May we become the wheat of Christ and be one pure bread. Grant this through Christ our Lord.

11. Jesus Is Nailed to the Cross   606
Ps 22:17f; Lk 23:34; Jn 6:38

THEY have pierced My hands and My feet; they have numbered all My bones.

Father, forgive them; for they do not know what they do.

It is not to do My own will that I have come down from heaven, but to do the will of Him Who sent Me.

Let us pray.

Heavenly Father, Your Son reconciled us to You and to one another. Help us to embrace His gift of grace and remain united with You. We ask this through Christ our Lord.

12. Jesus Dies on the Cross   613
Jn 12:32; Lk 23:46; Phil 2:8-9

ONCE I am lifted up from earth I will draw all people to Myself.

Father, into Your hands I commend My spirit.

He humbled Himself, obediently accepting even death, death on a cross! Because of this, God highly exalted Him.

Let us pray.

God our Father, by His Death Your Son has conquered death, and by His Resurrection He has given us life. Help us to adore His Death and embrace His Life. Grant this in the name of Jesus the Lord.

13. Jesus Is Taken Down from the Cross   624
Lk 24:26; Ps 119:165; 1 Jn 4:9f

DID not the Messiah have to suffer all of this so as to enter into His glory?

Those who love Your law have great peace.

God's love was revealed among us in this way: He sent His only Son to the world . . . as an offering for our sins.

Let us pray.

God our Father, grant that we may be associated in Christ's Death so that we may advance toward the resurrection with great hope. We ask this through Christ our Lord.

625

14. Jesus Is Placed in the Tomb
Jn 12:24; Rom 6:10-11; 1 Cor 15:4

U NLESS the grain of wheat falls to the ground and dies, it remains just a grain of wheat. But if it dies, it produces abundant fruit.

Christ's death was death to sin, once for all; his life is life for God. In the same way, you must consider yourselves dead to sin but alive for God in Christ Jesus.

Christ . . . in accordance with the Scriptures rose on the third day.

Let us pray.

Heavenly Father, You raised Jesus from the dead through Your Holy Spirit. Grant life to our mortal bodies through that same Spirit Who abides in us. We ask this in the name of Jesus the Lord.

624

Concluding Prayer

H EAVENLY Father, You delivered Your Son to the death of the Cross to save us from evil. Grant us the grace of the Resurrection. We ask this through Christ our Lord.

The Holy Bible   101-133

● *What is the Bible?*   101-104

The Bible is a collection of sacred books, which were composed under the positive influence of the Holy Spirit by men chosen by God, and which have been accepted by the Church as inspired.

● *Who is the principal author of the Bible?*   105

God is the principal author of the Bible.

● *When and where was the Bible written?*   106

The Bible was written at various times and in various places by men chosen for this purpose by God.

● *How many books are in the Bible?*   120

In the Bible, as we know it, there are seventy-three books; forty-six books are in the Old Testament and twenty-seven in the New Testament.

● *If the Bible is written by men, why do we say that it is the* 135 *Word of God?*

We say that the Bible is the Word of God because God inspired the men who wrote it.

● *Why is the Bible more excellent than any other book?*   134

The Bible is more excellent than any other book because God is its author and it centers around the mystery of the redemption of man.

● *How is the Old Testament related to the mystery of the re-* 121, 292 *demption?*

The Old Testament describes the remote preparation for the coming of the Messiah.

● *Who are some of the outstanding people of the Old Testa-* 59, 64 *ment?*   439

Abraham, our father in the faith; Moses, leader of God's people; David, King and Psalmist; and Isaiah, the Prophet of the Messiah.

● *How is the New Testament related to the mystery of the re-* 124, 292 *demption?*

The New Testament describes the nature of the Messiah and tells the story of His redemptive mission.

122, 869, 1227 • *Who are some of the outstanding people of the New Testament?*

Jesus Christ, the Son of God; Mary, His Virgin Mother; Peter, the Head of Christ's Church; and Paul, the Apostle who brought the Church to all people.

75, 80 • *What is Sacred Tradition?*

Sacred Tradition is the Word of God given to the Apostles by Christ and the Holy Spirit and handed down to their successors through the Church by means of prayer and Creeds, liturgical practices, and authoritative writings (Popes and bishops in union with the Holy Father).

1100-1102, 1190 • *Why is the Liturgy called the "Bible in action"?*

The Bible pervades every part of the liturgical rites of the Church. We find in this public worship biblical passages (Readings), biblical chants (Antiphons), biblical formulas (Greetings, Acclamations, and Institution Narrative), biblical allusions (Prayers), and biblical instruction (Homily).

For the Bible is God's Word to us and that it was first written with worship in mind. Indeed, it was the Word of God that formed God's people and that continues to do so today.

109, 113 • *How should we read the Bible?*

We should read the Bible with the mind of the Church who gave us the Bible and who interprets it for us. It will then become God's Word to us today.

The Catholic Church is the official interpreter of the Bible. As the people of God—both of the Old Covenant *in figure* and of the New Covenant *in reality*—she wrote the Sacred Scriptures. As the Church of Christ, she has interpreted them. And as the Church of Christians, she has always treasured them.

She encourages her members to study the Scriptures for she knows that they can discover nothing but what will make the Bible a greater force in their lives. And she knows that "ignorance of the Scriptures is ignorance of Christ."

See p. 62 for prayers before and after reading the Bible.

Divisions of the Old Testament

JEWISH O.T.	PROTESTANT O.T.	CATHOLIC O.T.
(24 books = 39)	(39 books)	(46 books)
The Torah (Law)	Historical Books	Historical Books
(5)	(17)	(21)
	(The Law)	(The Law)
Genesis	Genesis	Genesis
Exodus	Exodus	Exodus
Leviticus	Leviticus	Leviticus
Numbers	Numbers	Numbers
Deuteronomy	Deuteronomy	Deuteronomy
	Joshua	Joshua
The Prophets (8)	Judges	Judges
(Former)	Ruth	Ruth
	1 Samuel	1 Samuel
Joshua	2 Samuel	2 Samuel
Judges	1 Kings	1 Kings
Samuel (1 & 2)	2 Kings	2 Kings
Kings(1 & 2)	1 Chronicles	1 Chronicles
	2 Chronicles	2 Chronicles
(Latter)	Ezra	Ezra
Isaiah	Nehemiah	Nehemiah
Jeremiah	Esther	Tobit*
Ezekiel		Judith*
Prophets		Esther (parts)*
Hosea		1 Maccabees*
Joel		2 Maccabees*
Amos		
Obadiah	Wisdom Books (5)	Wisdom Books (7)
Micah	(The Writings)	(The Writings)
Jonah	Job	Job
Nahum	Psalms	Psalms
Habakkuk	Proverbs	Proverbs
Zephaniah	Qoheleth	Qoheleth
Haggai	Song of Songs	Song of Songs
Zechariah		Wisdom*
Malachi		Sirach*

Divisions of the Old Testament (Contd)

The Writings (11)	*Prophetic Books* (17) (The Prophets)	*Prophetic Books* (18) (The Prophets)
Chronicles (1 & 2)	Isaiah	Isaiah
Ezra-Nehemiah	Jeremiah	Jeremiah
Esther	Lamentations	Lamentations
Ruth		*Baruch**
Psalms	Ezekiel	Ezekiel
Proverbs	Daniel	Daniel *(parts)**
Job	Hosea	Hosea
Lamentations	Joel	Joel
Qoheleth	Amos	Amos
Song of Songs	Obadiah	Obadiah
Daniel	Jonah	Jonah
	Micah	Micah
	Nahum	Nahum
	Habakkuk	Habakkuk
	Zephaniah	Zephaniah
* Deuterocanonical Book (or parts)	Haggai	Haggai
	Zechariah	Zechariah
	Malachi	Malachi

120
Divisions of the New Testament

Historical Books (5)	*Didactic Books* (21)	*Prophetic Book* (1)
Matthew's Gospel	Romans	Revelation
Mark's Gospel	1 & 2 Corinthians	
Luke's Gospel	Galatians	
John's Gospel	Ephesians	
Acts of Apostles	Colossians	
	Philippians	
	Philemon	
	1 & 2 Thessalonians	
	1 & 2 Timothy	
	Titus	
	Hebrews	
	James	
	1 & 2 Peter	
	1, 2 & 3 John	
	Jude	

History of the Catholic Church in the United States

TABLE OF U.S. DATES AND EVENTS (1600-1900)

SECULAR AMERICAN HISTORY	AMERICAN CHURCH HISTORY
1607 Founding of Jamestown	1620 Oldest Marian shrine established in Florida
1649 Maryland Act of Toleration	1634 Maryland, first Catholic colony
1681 Religious toleration in Pennsylvania	1646 Martyrdom of St. Isaac Jogues
1704 The Boston News-Letter, first American newspaper	1697 Jesuit mission in California
	1756 Catholics number 7,000
1744 Start of King George's War (till 1763)	1767 First parish school (Philadelphia)
1754 Last French and Indian War	Jesuits expelled; Upper California missions entrusted to Franciscans
1765 Patrick Henry and the Stamp Act	
1774 First Continental Congress	1770 Bl. Junipero Serra in California
1775 Start of American Revolution	1785 Catholics number 25,000 among a population of 4 million
1776 Declaration of Independence	
1783 Treaty of Peace with England	1789 Constitutional religious freedom
1787 Writing of Constitution	Bishop Carroll of Baltimore
1790 Population 4 million	1789 Establishment of Georgetown, first Catholic College in U.S.
1791 Bill of Rights takes effect	
1803 Louisiana Purchase	1791 Baltimore Sulpician Seminary
1812 War with England (till 1814)	1808 Baltimore is made archdiocese
1819 Purchase of Florida	1820 Trusteeism
1823 Monroe Doctrine	1823 United States Miscellany, first Catholic newspaper
1844 Invention of telegraph	
1846 War with Mexico (till 1848)	1839 Trusteeism overcome in New York
1848 Start of California Gold Rush	1852 First Plenary Council of Baltimore
1853 Know-Nothing movement	1866 Second Plenary Council of Baltimore
1861 Start of Civil War (to 1865)	1875 First American Cardinal, John McCloskey Archbishop of New York
1863 Emancipation of slaves	
1867 Purchase of Alaska	1876 Faith of Our Fathers published
1870 Blacks obtain suffrage	1879 St. Patrick's Cathedral is completed
1876 Invention of telephone	1882 Knights of Columbus founded
1886 American Federation of Labor (AFL) founded	1884 Third Plenary Council of Baltimore
	1885 Appearance of Baltimore Catechism
1894 Labor Day established	1889 Founding of Catholic University
1898 Annexation of Hawaii War with Spain	1890 Archbishop John Ireland addresses the National Education Association about public and private schools
	1893 The Apostolic Delegation is established in Washington, D.C.

90

TABLE OF U.S. DATES AND EVENTS (1900-1990)

SECULAR AMERICAN HISTORY

1901 Assassination of President William McKinley

1902 Coal strike by United Mine Workers

1906 San Francisco earthquake

1912 Sinking of the "Titanic"

1917 U.S. enters World War I (till 1918)
Start of Prohibition

1919 Strike of steel workers

1920 Women obtain suffrage

1921 First immigration restriction law passed by Congress

1925 Beginning of golden age of radio broadcasting

1929 Stock market crash

1930 Decade of the Great Depression

1933 FDR starts the first four terms as President
End of Prohibition

1935 Formation of the Congress of Industrial Organizations (CIO)

1941 U.S. enters World War II (till 1945)

1945 U.S. becomes charter member of UN
First atom bomb produced

1948 Start of television era

1950 Start of Korean War (till 1953)

1952 First hydrogen bomb exploded

1959 Alaska and Hawaii admitted as States

1963 Assassination of President Kennedy

1968 Assassination of Martin Luther King

1969 U.S. astronauts walk on the moon

1973 Supreme Court overturns laws against abortion

1974 Resignation of President Richard Nixon

1976 Bicentennial celebration

1979 American hostages taken by Iran

1983 Invasion of Grenada to oust leftists

1986 Space Shuttle Challenger explodes, killing 7 on board

1987 New era of glasnost (openness) between U.S. and Russia

AMERICAN CHURCH HISTORY

1904 Founding of National Catholic Educational Association

1905 Founding of the Extension Society

1908 Catholic Church in U.S. removed from jurisdiction of Congregation for the Propagation of the Faith

1909 America, a national Catholic weekly is founded by the Jesuits

1911 Establishment of the Catholic Foreign Mission Society (Maryknoll)

1917 National Catholic War Council

1919 National Catholic Welfare Council

1919 Alfred E. Smith becomes first elected Catholic governor

1926 28th International Eucharistic Congress is held in Chicago

1931 Monsignor Fulton J. Sheen begins his celebrated preaching career on the NBC Catholic Hour program

1940 First Liturgical Week held

1946 St. Frances Xavier Cabrini becomes first U.S. citizen saint

1947 Opening of School of Liturgical Studies at Notre Dame (first liturgical institute in world)

1952 Supreme Court approves Released Time Program

1959 Catholics become largest religious group in U.S. Congress (twelve senators, ninety-one representatives)

1960 John F. Kennedy becomes first Catholic President

1965 Paul VI visits the UN and New York

1966 Establishment of National Conference of Catholic Bishops

1970 Publication of New American Bible, first American Catholic translation from the original languages

1979 Visit of John Paul II to U.S.

1987 Second visit of John Paul II

How Do Catholics Minister to One Another?

1. **Ministry Defined:** from the Greek—serving and attending upon someone: (A) grace-filled actions; (B) service to people; (C) living the Holy Spirit. 874-959, 1142

2. **Universal:** There is neither Jew nor Greek, there is neither slave nor free, there is no male or female in Christ.

3. Gifts and talents shared, with, for, and through the Church community.

4. Guided by the abiding presence of the Holy Spirit.

5. Ministries other than priests and religious:

Permanent Diaconate	Chancellor	Parish Council
Tribunals	Greeter	Usher
Married state	Sodalist	Counselor
Single state	Acolyte	Adult Ed. Teacher
Lector	Corporator	Prison Ministry
Health Care Minister	Cantor	Catechist
RCIA Sponsor	Child Care	Altar Server
Seminary Faculty	Choir	Rel. Education
Eucharistic Minister	Pastoral Associate	Music Minister

Catholics and Their Relationship with the World

1. Catholics are aware of and speak out against injustices in government, workplace, community, and the home.

2. Catholics publicly stand for the protection and quality of life for all people, especially the unborn, the handicaped, the sick, the bereaved, and the elderly.

3. Catholics take responsibility for the poor, rejected, outcasts of society, and those who are considered to be members of minority groups.

4. Catholics lobby for a living wage, safe and wholesome working conditions, while, at the same time, decrying sexual harassment and abuse, especially in the workplace, the community, and the home.

5. Catholic couples seek personal holiness through living and promoting value-oriented family life and assuming responsibility for educating and protecting the faith of their children.

6. Civil divorce does not alienate Catholics from the sacramental life of the Church, unless one would remarry without benefit of an annulment, which, in cases where, after serious and broad study, the Church declares a true marriage bond never existed.

7. Given the pain of separation and divorce, the Catholic faith community provides pastoral care so that people in distress feel fully loved and accepted by the faith community.

8. Pastoral care of widows and individuals called to the single state is exercised in such a manner as to make every individual welcomed, acknowledged, and accepted for his/her unique contributions to the faith community.

Why Do Catholics Consider Themselves a Christ-Centered People?

1691,
1698.
1716.
1878,
1897,
1929

1. In Jesus, we see "the image of the invisible God," (Col 1:15)—the perfect human being.

2. Jesus gives divine likeness to sons and daughters of Adam.

3. Jesus worked with human hands, thought with a human mind, acted by human choice, and loved with a human heart.

4. We accept all people as having dignity and intelligence.

5. All are called to a relationship with God through Christ.

6. All are, through Jesus, called to happiness with God.

7. Hope for immortal life highlights the need to be Christ-centered in our times:

    (A) To live according to God's word and will.
    (B) To make Jesus, through our lives, present to the world.
    (C) To live a lively and mature faith.
    (D) To be defenders of the depressed, homeless, and rejected.
    (E) To stand against hunger, poverty, war, and all injustice.
    (F) To share our abundance.
    (G) To be in solidarity with those confined to nursing homes, hospitals, and jails.
    (H) To speak for value-oriented processes in our civic communities.
    (I) To be concerned for the common welfare of all.
    (J) To protect the rights of the unborn, the unconscious sick and elderly, and the severely handicapped.

8. We are a countercultural people.

Evangelization in the Church

1. Definition: we are called as Church "to proclaim the reign of God" (Mk 1:15):
   (A) to the unchurched in our land; (B) to the unchurched in other cultures; (C) to those already committed to the Gospel.

2. A call to all the Baptized to share their gift and the Good News:

active parish lives	Liturgy (Mass) as community
Scripture study	community interaction
prayer groups	public faith witness

3. The Rite of Christian Initiation of Adults (RCIA):
   (A) Modern adaptation of ancient process of becoming part of the Catholic Faith community (Church).
   (B) Learning and embracing the Faith step by step.
   (C) Catechumen (Unbaptized), and Candidate (Baptized) introduced to history, tradition, and theology of the Church.
   (D) Prayer, experience, and life in the parish.

4. Forms people willing to live as responsible Catholics:
   (A) Liturgical celebration.
   (B) Small group sharing and instruction.
   (C) Community concern and support.

5. Who may benefit?
   (A) People of other faiths wishing full communion with Roman Catholics.
   (B) Non-Catholics married to Catholics.
   (C) People with no religious affiliation wishing to investigate faith issues in a welcoming, celebrating atmosphere.

95

Why Are Catholics Ecumenical in Spirit?

839, 849, 2044

1. Strong in their Faith.

2. Profound respect for others' beliefs and experiences of God in their lives.

3. Cooperation in fundamental societal values for the common good.

4. Acknowledgment and appreciation for the Jewish religion in which Christianity is deeply rooted.

5. Seek to advance elements of other faiths that unify all religions.

What Should Twenty-First Century Catholics Look Like?

767, 1694, 2442- 2449, 2697

1. Men and women with a firm belief in Jesus and a willingness to share His mission in the world.

2. Men and women of prayer, integrity, and generosity of spirit.

3. Men and women concerned for justice for all segments of society.

4. Men and women who live the forgiveness of the Gospel of Jesus Christ.

5. Men and women concerned for the poor, the sick, the disabled, the elderly, the disenfranchised, the unborn, and the weak.

6. Men and women of peace.

7. Men and women outstanding in their allegiance to and their work with the poor.

8. Men and women assuming the responsibility for vibrant parish communities, top-notch Catholic, value-oriented schools, and parish-wide catechesis.

9. Men and women generous with their God-given talents for the benefit of the Kingdom here and hereafter.

10. Men and women striving for perfection in the Lord and leading others to eternal salvation.